C000141144

This Is Coffee Point: Go Ahead

Alaska Pioneer Series
Memoirs and personal histories of Alaska pioneers.

- ***Home Sweet Homestead:*** *Sketches of Pioneer Life in Interior Alaska,* Joy Griffin, 1995
- ***This Is Coffee Point: Go Ahead:*** *A Mother's Story of Fishing & Survival at Alaska's Bristol Bay,* Wilma Williams, 1995
- ***If You've Got It To Do—Get On With It:*** *A Family Settles the Early Town of Homer, Alaska,* Wilma Williams, 1996

This Is Coffee Point: Go Ahead

A Mother's Story of Fishing &
Survival at Alaska's Bristol Bay

Wilma Williams

Copyright © 2014 by Wilma Williams.

ISBN:	Softcover	978-1-4990-1012-1
	eBook	978-1-4990-1011-4

All rights reserved. No part of this book may be reproduced or transmitted in any form or by any means, electronic or mechanical, including photocopying, recording, or by any information storage and retrieval system, without permission in writing from the copyright owner.

Any people depicted in stock imagery provided by Thinkstock are models, and such images are being used for illustrative purposes only.
Certain stock imagery © Thinkstock.

This book was printed in the United States of America.

Rev. date: 04/28/2014

To order additional copies of this book, contact:
Xlibris LLC
1-888-795-4274
www.Xlibris.com
Orders@Xlibris.com
540722

Contents

PART TWO: COFFEE POINT

This book is dedicated to my son Tommy,
without whom these experiences
at the bay would never have happened.
Tommy lived every moment of his allotted time to the fullest,
leaving behind wonderful memories
for both family and friends.

Acknowledgements

First, I would like to thank Jackie Vaughn who spent many hours reading my stories. She is a good enough friend to say "that doesn't sound right"—and get away with it.

Thanks to the Homer Writer's Group who supported me all the way, letting me learn from them as they read their stories and critiqued mine.

To Professor Beth Graber, under whose gentle guidance I learned many things, I offer my thankfulness.

And to Diane Ford Wood, my editor, publisher and friend: We have butted heads many times but I have never doubted her abilities. In the end, it is to her I owe a great deal of gratitude and appreciation.

Foreword

I was only eight months old in 1926 when, after much tedious traveling, my family landed by boat in Seldovia, Alaska.

But I was not destined to stay.

Soon after our arrival, my mother became ill. Frightened, Dad sent us to the states where she could get proper medical attention.

It would be a long time before I would see Alaska again. When I did, I would fight the return with all the drama and vigor a fifteen year-old could muster. In the end, it was the beauty and wonder of the state that won me over.

When I was 19, I married my first husband, Lloyd, in Homer, Alaska. During our turbulent 18 years together, we had five children and adopted Carolee. By the time we fished the bay, Carolee's life was set in another direction and she never fished with us.

In 1963, I married Charlie Williams, a local fisherman and bachelor, and from the start, our lives took on a nautical flavor. For the most part, I was very happy with Charlie. He was good to my kids, and our future together looked bright.

My Son—Where Are You?

Powerful gray clouds swirled restlessly over the busy Bristol Bay fishing fleet. It was July 1974, and from my kitchen window, I watched the tides move in, the winds pick up, and some of the smaller boats head in for safety.

As I put a meal together for my family in this, our tenth season at the bay, I listened on the VHF radio for news of the catch. My husband, Charlie, was already delivering his salmon. But Tommy, my oldest son, was still out there—hopeful of beating Charlie's catch record.

From atop my warming oven, the radio was alive with fishermen making arrangements to unload. I was just taking the scalloped potatoes from the oven when Charlie called.

"Coffee Point, this is *Beach Runner*."

"This is Coffee Point. Go ahead, honey."

"Wilma, have you heard from Tom lately? I don't see the *Rebel* any place, and it's getting pretty rough out there."

Prickly chills raised goose bumps on my arms, even in my warm kitchen. In Alaska, all the fishing families knew the dangers, but we rarely talked about them.

"I'll give Tom a call from up here and see if I can get an answer."

A worried sounding "Roger" came back.

"Calling the *Rebel*, calling the *Rebel*. This is Coffee Point. Have you got the radio on, Tom?"

I was answered by silence, very unusual for that time of year. Other fishermen were listening, I knew—listening, waiting and watching.

Charlie's voice came on again. "I'm going to take a run down to Bishop Creek. I may be able to see him from there."

"That's a Roger, *Beach Runner*."

"Coffee Point, this is the *Brown Bear*."

"Go ahead, *Brown Bear*."

"I just picked up a gas can off Bishop Creek. It had '*Rebel*' written in black letters on the side of it."

Only that morning I had seen Tom fill that can and put it in his skiff. Be calm, Wilma.

My hands shook as I pressed down the mike button.

"Roger, thanks for the info, *Brown Bear*. Did you copy, *Beach Runner?*"

"Yeah, I got it," answered Charlie.

It was time, I knew, to get everyone involved.

"Alert! Alert! This is Coffee Point. Be on the lookout for a gray 20-foot skiff; name on the bow is *Rebel*; one person aboard."

I broke for a minute as I turned off the oven, scooted the potatoes back into it, and grabbed my coat.

"I am switching to my handheld," I said into the mike. "But I'll continue to stand by on this frequency."

I grabbed the little palm-sized radio and raced out to my truck—an International Suburban that had seen better days. A mile down the beach, I saw Charlie's rig parked at Red and Margaret's house. I drove over to it and stopped. My heart felt like a trip hamer.

Oh, my son—Where are you?

As I started into the house, my radio came to life.

"Coffee Point, we have a line on a capsized gray skiff. We picked it up down by the light at Bishop Creek."

"Roger—Is there any sign of Tom?"

"Negative, negative. But we'll drop the skiff off at the point."

"That's a Roger. Give a call when you are close," I answered weakly.

Snapping off the radio, I headed for home. Forgetting the Suburban, I ran blindly toward the point, not wanting to hear what was coming next. Somewhere behind me, Charlie called to me. Ignoring him, I continued to run.

I will not let them tell me they found TomTom in those cold, angry, thrashing waves.

I ran faster to the shoreline where the damp sand made it easier to move. Right in front of me, a boat was coming ashore. Someone sitting on the bow jumped into the water; I stopped in my tracks.

"Mom, Mom," the person called to me.

Wet, bedraggled, wonderful arms were around me. I touched Tommy's face. It was hard to see through the tears, but I looked at him a minute—and then I shouted at him: "How dare you almost drown! You nearly scared me to death!"

My son hugged me tighter. "Well, Mom, I wasn't real crazy about it either."

PART ONE

ALONG THE BEACH

Bristol Bay Long Johns

In the fall of 1963, Tommy burst into our house in Homer, Alaska, and announced:

"Mom, Homie next door went to Bristol Bay this year and made money fishing. I'd like to go next year."

I thought for a moment, realizing that with TomTom, you never said "You are too young to do that."

"Hmm . . . It's a long time till spring; we can talk about that later. Get me a bucket of coal now, would you honey?"

Meanwhile, I filed the request under "Tommy's Bright Ideas" and assumed he would soon forget it.

Wrong.

One day, as I made out an order for kids' winter clothes from the Sears catalog, Tommy hung over my shoulder watching.

"Mom, when you order my long johns, be sure and get them a size bigger."

"Why, honey?" I asked.

"So I can wear them out to Bristol Bay next summer. Homie says it gets pretty cold on those night fish picks."

Oops . . . That idea is still floating around? Well—what harm can come from getting his long johns a little big this year?

In January, Tommy brought the subject up again.

"Mom, could you get the forms for my fishing license for Bristol Bay? I don't want any last-minute hang-ups."

He looked at me, waiting for an answer.

"And would you write to the people that Homie fished for?"

I was on the spot.

"Tommy, you are only 12—It would be gross negligence for me to let you go where there is hardly any communication and where I wouldn't know if you are being fed."

"Mom, I need to make money and I don't want to become a full-grown paper boy as an occupation!"

He had a point there.

In the end, I promised to ask Homie's mother for more information. But I knew this would only get me off the hook for a couple of days.

Sensing my reluctance, Tommy applied for his fishing license himself, paying for it with money from his paper route. Finally, I had to give him some kind of an answer.

"Okay, Tom, I'll make you a deal," I told him. "I found out the name and address of the employer at Bristol Bay. I will write to him, and if he'll take all of us, we'll go. If he won't, no more discussion on the matter—deal?"

TomTom grinned and hugged me.

"You'll see, Mom. It'll be just fine."

His exuberance made me feel a little guilty. I didn't think any sane person would take on a 37-year-old woman with a half-dozen kids.

Charlie, my new husband, gave his reluctant blessing to the idea, but he wouldn't be able to come with us. He was already committed to fishing Cook Inlet that season. Our town was low on jobs, and we both liked the double shot at winter groceries.

By early spring, we hadn't heard anything new and I felt comfortable that the issue was resolved. In March, the Great Alaska Earthquake hit, causing great destruction and sending many Alaskans into a flurry. Tommy, forever the optimist, was still single-minded, setting aside things like a pocket knife and a small hatchet to carry with him to the bay.

The Redheaded Stranger

It was a cold April in Homer and the water supply to our kitchen sink had stopped. Grabbing a blow torch, I crawled under the house to hunt for the frozen pipe. Above me, the kids were instructed to tap once on the floor if the water started to run, and twice if it didn't.

As I moved around in the cold dirt trying to locate the problem, the tapping went back and forth with regularity—then stopped.

Darn! Where have those kids gone?

With the blow torch still alive in my hand, I dragged myself out and found the kids talking to a stocky, redheaded stranger. Flashing a winning smile, the man introduced himself:

"Hello. I'm Clair Clark. You wrote me about fishing a set-net at Bristol Bay. I'm in Homer on business and thought I'd stop by to see if you're the type of people who can handle a net."

Pointing to the flaming instrument in my hand, he laughed and said, "I guess you'll do!"

Although we didn't know it at the time, that meeting established a pattern that would change our lives forever.

A Broad, Sandy Beach

Tommy picking fish the first season

Tommy got his wish: we were all to report to Bristol Bay to fish. On June 10, 1964, I kissed a concerned Charlie good-bye. Carrying 16-month old David in my arms, I followed my other five children aboard the plane to King Salmon, our first stop.

The flight was beautiful and the kids chattered happily among themselves. At King Salmon we switched to a plane equipped with big tires for beach landings, and continued to Big Creek camp. It was hard to believe that an airplane, stuffed with so many people and a pickup load of gear, could actually set down on a beach in the middle of nowhere.

Looking us over, pilot George Tibbetts, Sr., said: "If you ever need help getting out of here, let me know."

He probably thought I had bitten off more than I could chew—or did he know something I didn't?

When we arrived, Clair, the man we'd talked to in Homer, met us in a 4-by-4 truck. His crew tried to take the tent house we would live in across the creek to our fishing sites, but ran into trouble. So that night, we stayed at Clair's camp, which consisted of several houses, tents, and a main cookhouse. After a wholesome meal, Carmen, 12, and the other children went to play with the local kids, as I settled tired little David down for the night.

In the morning, we were shocked to see our future home, the tent house, moved about a mile out on the sand flats by the tides. But Clair's crew didn't seem worried about it. They just dragged out two replacements, hooked them to a truck and tractor, and led us on a one-mile trek to where we would fish. As we traveled, we had to be careful about how we breathed or talked or we'd end up sucking mosquitoes into our lungs.

Passing fishing sites nearly every 300 feet, Clair finally stopped the procession and asked me:

"Where would you like to live?"

I looked around. "Where are our fishing sites?"

He pointed them out.

Turning away from the bay, I climbed the sand burm on the high beach. From there, I could see a lovely little lake shimmering in the morning sun, alive with wildlife. Rising from the water, white swans flapped huge wings, baby ptarmigans scurried through the grass at my feet, and in the distance, a Sandhill crane flew up from the muskeg.

Turning back to the bay, I noticed that the beach was broad, sandy and beautiful at this spot.

"This will be just fine," I answered.

After the trucks set the two skid-mounted tents on the sand back of the shoreline, we were left alone in our new world.

The quiet was so powerful, you could almost hear it. What a wonderful feeling of tranquility it inspired, even if we were dead tired.

Precious Times

Over the next few days, we rolled up our sleeves and prepared to make our new home more comfortable. In the sleep tent, equipped with two double-decker bunks, the children unrolled sleeping bags and scooted their duffel bags underneath for easy access. Coni, my 15-year-old daughter, bunked with me in the cookhouse tent where two cots doubled as benches. Tammy, 10, and Terrill, 9, had already placed a bouquet of colorful tundra flowers on the little plywood table for us to enjoy.

On that first day, I located the grocery box and got out moosemeat for sandwiches, some cinnamon rolls, and canned soup. From the lake, we pulled water to boil for drinking, and we all sat down on the two benches and enjoyed our first meal.

After lunch, I pulled some gas cans from their case and nailed the wooden case to the tent frame as a cupboard for butter and dishes. Later, using more cases, I fashioned additional cupboards and chairs. Using beachcombed plywood, I built a drainboard, and for a sink, I cut up a rectangular five-gallon gas can, attaching a small piece of hose to allow the water to drain out to the sand.

We also needed an oven, so I cut up another gas can and threaded wire back and forth through the sides for a rack.

House Beautiful never asked to photograph our kitchen, but it looked just lovely to us!

The barren landscape gave little privacy from the planes flying overhead at every hour, making our need for an outhouse even more critical. We searched the tides for driftwood, but we needed something heavier for stability. This was solved when we found a boat hatch cover on the beach, about a mile from our camp. By its weight, I would say it came from the *Queen Mary*, but it was really only about 3-by-6. It was so heavy that even with all of us tugging, we had to move it in shifts. With all our strength, we'd drag it as far as we could, return to camp for a while, and then come back and try again later. After three trips, we finally got it home.

After we figured out where we wanted our new outhouse, Tommy dug the hole. Propping the oblong-shaped hatch on one end, I played carpenter. Using castaway fishing signs and canvas, we built two sides and a door. As a final touch, we nailed a coffee can to the wall as a toilet paper holder.

What a luxury—we had a marvelous, private bathroom!

With each day's work completed, I would curl up on my bed and write a story to read to the children the next day. Usually I did this by candlelight so I wouldn't disturb Coni. Afterwards, I would read Charlie's letters; I missed him terribly. But I also knew that these were beautiful, golden times with my children that would always be precious to me. Remembering this made all the sacrifices easier to bear.

Fear Gripped My Heart

Rumor has it that during World War II, a one-man Japanese submarine landed on our beach. The operator got out, looked around, and sailed away—there wasn't much to see.

Things hadn't changed much since then. Except for fishing sites, the shoreline was deserted nearly all the way from Big Creek to Bishop Creek. We had no trucks or telephones in those days, and for cooking and lights, we relied on a Coleman™ stove and gas lamps. Without vehicles, we set all our nets by hand. This came easily because of our experiences fishing Cook Inlet two years before.

The day after we got settled at the beach, Clair's crew dropped off our nets and installed the stakes our nets would be attached to. At the first opportunity to fish, Tommy, Coni and I carried the corks and leads, while the little ones (not wanting to be left out), carried the middle of the net. Like a giant caterpillar, we walked to the top stake where we would attach it to the headline. Then two of us would pick up the outside end of the net, one on the leads, one on the corks, picking up a good handful of gear, and walk toward the outside buoy to attach the net's other end. When it got hard to pull, the next two would do the same thing until we had the net set, ready for the incoming tide to bring us fish. When it was time to pick fish, we picked by hand in the mud.

That year, we fished two sites, but within a short time, the number grew to four.

As we worked, we all prayed for a fishing season good enough to cover our overhead and net us a profit. From the beginning, we had a work plan. Everyone would be paid between $50 and $100 for the season. Terrill had the water detail, carrying it in small buckets from the lake. Tammy carried messages between the house and the beach and helped Carmen with the babysitting and cooking.

We all shared the washing, and even little Terrill scrubbed his own socks on the washboard. For a clothesline, we staked poles left by the tides and strung a line between them. The winds at Bristol Bay certainly demanded attention and, if we were foolish enough to leave a sheet on the line at night, by morning it would be whipped until the edges were frayed, or we'd find it dragging in the swamp behind the house—a soggy, muddy mess.

By late June as the fishing picked up, our days took on a pattern. We set gear, pulled gear, picked fish, delivered fish, ate, and slept.

The Alaska Department of Fish & Game, the state agency that determined when we could fish, was a very exacting force in those years. They would fly overhead the last minute before an "opening" (times when we were allowed to fish), daring us, it felt, to put one mesh of gear in the water early.

Openings were usually scheduled just before the tide came in, which gave us barely enough time to set our nets dry. The idea was to give us a fair chance at the fish before the drift boats, sitting just offshore, swooped them up in their nets. We all knew the rules and they were strictly enforced.

But one morning, a near-disaster struck that, even after all these years, still scares me to think about. A morning opening was scheduled and, according to my watch, the kids and I were on the beach early. As we got everything ready, I looked around, wondering where the other setnetters were. At 9 a.m., the tides were right to fish, but as we set out our first net, no one else was on the beach. Finally, I sent Tammy and Terrill a quarter mile away to another fisherman's cabin.

Soon, they came running back with the two neighbors. "Mom! Fish & Game gave us a bum set-out time; we are exactly one hour early!"

Fear gripped my heart. The combination of Fish & Game misjudging the tides, and me setting my watch in the dark, had just made a lawbreaker out of me. I was sure I would go to jail, be fined, and they would take my kids away. Our neighbors offered to help pull the net out of the water, and we all tried, but it was too late—the tide was running strong.

Suddenly, my practical side took over and I started shouting orders: "Tom, get us a line, hook it to that other buoy, and play it out to shore.

Terrill, run and get the shovels. Tam and Carmen, roll that short piece of log down the bank. We are going to set the other site." Perhaps, I figured, the money from a legal set would feed my children while I was in jail.

As the kids ran in every direction, a small Fish & Game plane landed down the beach. I knew these would be the people who would take me to prison. I spoke to the kids as calmly as I could:

"Look busy. Just straighten that other net out and get ready to tie on. Coni, if they take me away, you are in charge. You kids keep fishing. You have a job to do."

I sneaked a peek at our illegal net; the fish were happily turning flips over the cork line. Ordinarily this sight would bring great joy to my heart, but not that day.

Down the beach, I could see the Fish & Game officer inspecting an abandoned net full of spoiled fish left by another fisherman. When the officer was done, instead of coming toward us, he returned to his plane, revved the engine, and flew away. In a state of shock, the kids ran to hug me, but the fish were still running and we had to set the gear. In the end, we had a decent catch of over 800 fish in the first net, and 400 in the second and it made over season.

One beautiful evening, when the children were tucked in bed after a hard day of fishing, I sat on the beach looking out over the bay. Since we'd been there, I'd watched my children get brown, work together, and help each other to attain our goals. They were busy, happy, and learning new things. I decided to do whatever I had to make fishing the bay a yearly project after that.

Wilma and Tommy collecting Japanese glass floats the first season

The Feast

By late June, my record book showed that our bills were paid—and that called for a celebration! Until then, we had been living on simple rations of soup, sandwiches, cereal and moose stew in order to get into the black.

In preparation for the party, the kids and I walked the mile and a half to Clair's camp store to buy chicken, real butter, potatoes, and fruit drink mix. The latter would make the swampwater we drank taste a little better. The feast was such a success, we named it the "Breaking into the Black Feast," and it became a yearly ritual.

The Bear's Prize

"Hey, Wilma. There's a big seal out on the sandbar by Big Creek. Do you want to go skin him?"

I stopped picking fish long enough to answer the boys in the camp truck.

"You betcha, just as soon as we get through here," I hollered.

I tried to act like I knew what I was doing, but I had never skinned anything before. I had seen marvelous stools, jackets, even bikinis made from seal skin, and I wanted that hide.

As the sun's last rays flared up along the western horizon, Tom, Tam, Terrill and I set out on our seal-skinning adventure. Armed with a butcher knife and a hunting knife, we searched the sandflats for the tell-tale lump. After a mile or so, we saw the seal far out on the bar.

Although it was sunset, we knew July was never very dark in Alaska. But I still worried about finding our way back. A plan wouldn't hurt, I decided, so I called out to the children: "I think we'll follow the beach to the point at Big Creek, and then head out to the seal on the flats." This would allow us to use the silhouette of the navigation marker on the point as a definite landmark for our return journey.

When we reached the carcass, it was the biggest I'd ever seen. Charlie, who grew up around these things, would have known what type of knife to use, but we just used what we'd brought along. We worked hard for a couple of hours, and in our caution not to damage the hide, we left a lot of heavy fat on it. It took all four of us to carry it, as we followed our earlier tracks along the beach.

Nearing the turn toward home, Tommy and I, who carried the front two corners of the hide, stopped abruptly. We all stared down at the huge bear tracks marked across our previous footprints. Apparently the animal had observed us, and retreated back toward the creek. We had been blissfully unaware of his presence.

Keeping our eyes on the high grass along the shoreline, we panted heavily under our burden, trying to sing to make our presence known. We mustered the most enthusiasm for *Jesus Loves Me,* hoping desperately that someone upstairs was listening and watching over us right then.

As we walked along in the half-light, our eyes played tricks on us: Scattered along the upper beach, rusty barrel buoys seemed to be moving. Finally, I said to Tommy, "Maybe we should just give the bear the hide."

"What good would that do, Mom? We smell more like the seal than the seal does."

And of course, he was right.

It was after midnight when we rolled up the hide and stuck it in a barrel by the tenthouses. Through the whole ordeal, none of the kids even whimpered, but I knew how scared they were. They just kept at it, tugging and hiking for home.

When we got back, Coni and Carmen prepared hot cocoa and a pot of hot water for washing up, wrinkling their noses at how we smelled. Once the kids were in bed, I drank some peppermint tea and thanked the Guy Upstairs for His protection on that nerve-wracking journey.

The next morning, Tommy fleshed out the hide, stretched it on a board, and set it up against the tenthouse to cure. But the seal was a prize that was not ours to keep. That night, our friendly brown bear finally claimed his prey, scattering Tommy's plywood frame in pieces across the swamp.

Although there were some disappointments that first season, it was a happy bunch that headed home with an $1,800 paycheck. Since our expenses were low, we thought it was a good amount for one month's work, and the experience fishing together had been priceless.

Coming Around Again

When we arrived back in Homer after our first season at the bay, Charlie greeted us with open arms; it felt good to be home again.

As fall neared, I put away the smoked fish we'd canned, Charlie went moose hunting, and the kids returned to school. About that time, Coni took an important step in her young life, marrying a responsible, boyish-looking schoolmate from Homer named Mike DeVaney.

When spring came, Coni and I coaxed our husbands to come with us to the bay the next season. To entice them, we told them about the beautiful weather and good fishing conditions. There were enough fish to make it worthwhile, we told them, and there was no bull kelp to interfere with the nets like in Kachemak Bay. Finally, Charlie and Mike agreed.

But nothing went the way we described.

Four days before it was time to leave for the season, Coni gave birth to little Lance. She was still recovering when we left and, feeling protective of her, I was disappointed to find that our flight reservations in King Salmon were ignored and the big canneries had tied up all the planes. After waiting hours, we were the last ones to leave the terminal.

Once at the sites, we moved into tents while we built a cabin. The wind blew and the rain came down in sheets. But worst of all, there were so many fish, the canneries ran out of cans and could no longer accept our catch. I am sure that both Charlie and Mike thought we had intentionally dragged them to the gates of hell.

Another problem we'd forgotten to mention was the mud. Ten fathoms out on our net, it would reach the top of our knee boots. Unless we hand-pulled the net ashore on the water, and then reset it after picking the fish, we had to carry every fish back to the shoreline through an insufferable deluge of mud. Add to that the gusty winds and pelting, stinging rain, and it was clear we earned our money. Soaking wet and chilled to the bone, my kids did their jobs without complaining. I wonder if I ever told them how proud I was of them.

But life at the bay wasn't all drudgery. Each day, after the fish were delivered and the nets stacked, those kids could still manage to giggle about something funny as we sipped hot cocoa or tea to warm us up before bed.

On occasional lazy days, the children would lie on the beach, play ball, or splash in the warm tide pools. Mike and Tommy rigged a plank between two gas barrels, and the kids made a few hair-raising trips into the surf with it. The only one who didn't participate was Coni's little Lance—his outings were usually enjoyed from a pack on one of our backs.

By the end of the season, July 20th that year, we netted a whopping $10,000. It was enough to pay the bills, put some in the bank, and even buy a few extras. In Anchorage, we bought a black Chevy convertible with red interior and I bought a scarf and dark glasses; we were off to watch the local hot rod races.

The Pink Trailer

Winter jobs were scarce in Homer, so we decided to look for work on Kodiak Island. In those days, it was a wide-open boom town with lots of money floating around.

In August, we all boarded the *Tustumena* for the eighteen hour trip to Kodiak. Only Tommy wasn't coming; he was enrolled in the Catholic school in Copper Valley and was busy preparing to leave.

Within two days, Charlie went crab fishing on the *Thomas-J* and I found work at Alaska Packer's Cannery as floor lady in charge of about 50 girls. We had a good crew, I enjoyed the job, and working made the days go by faster while Charlie was out fishing.

The original cannery building, which had been destroyed by the tidal wave that followed the 1964 earthquake, was replaced by a beached ship. Aboard were 105 employees, including the cooking and butchering crews. We worked sixty hours a week, trying to keep up with the full-to-the-brim crab boats tied two and three deep at the dock. Things moved fast because the fishermen were anxious to go back out for another load.

For living space, Coni and Mike brought their trailer, parking it in Jackson's Trailer Park. After a big search, Charlie and I found a one-bedroom house to rent, but with so many of us, it was very crowded.

Grocery shopping one day, I looked up to see Tessie Scroggs, a friend from Homer. As we shopped, we chatted, and I bemoaned the fact that we were all squeezed into such a small house.

"We have a three-bedroom house trailer in Seattle that we would like to sell," she told me.

It sounded interesting. I thought on it, and somewhere between the fresh vegetables and meat, I said:

"Tessie—it will take a little while to put together the freight money and talk to Charlie, but I'm sure the trailer is a done deal if you will carry the papers."

As we paid for our groceries we discussed terms, and I promised to get back to her when I had the freight money together. Since Charlie was fishing at the south end of the island, the plan was not yet "husband-approved." But I figured the money he earned on his trip could pay the freight on the trailer, and Tessie could arrange for it to be loaded on a boat headed north after that.

Three weeks later, when Charlie was on his way in from fishing, I called Tessie to get the trailer project going.

Her answer floored me: "Oh, I knew that you needed the trailer and would figure out the money, so I had it loaded on the freighter docking here tomorrow."

Although I am prone to doing my own thinking, I hadn't said a word about the trailer to Charlie. Now I had to figure out how to tell him about what I had purchased—sight-unseen.

By the time Charlie got home, I was pretty nervous, and the evening slipped away with no opportunity to talk. The next morning, still in the dilemma, I decided to jump in with both feet:

"Hey everyone, it's a beautiful day. Let's go for a ride."

Kodiak has few roads, and Charlie automatically chose the one that took us past the docks. As we drove along the hillside overlooking the bay, I could see the freighter—huge and impressive—with two house trailers sitting topside.

"Oh, look at the trailers," I said nonchalantly.

"Yeah, I sure wish one of them was ours," Charlie said, observing them.

Good reaction so far.

"If you had your choice, which one would you want honey?" I asked carefully.

Laughing at my silly game, he answered: "Oh, I guess the pink one."

"Well that's good," I said, "because that one is ours!"

Suddenly I had Charlie's undivided attention. As he slammed on the brakes, the kids started hollering, and everyone began talking at once about where to put it, how to get it there, and when could we move in.

Charlie was pleased—and I was relieved. By the end of the week, our new trailer was safely set up in Jackson's Trailer Park, not far from Mike and Coni.

After the trailer freight charges, our bank account sank to perilous depths. We also discovered that heating the trailer with electricity cost about half my monthly wages. As a solution, I talked my way into an oil furnace on credit, so I could keep the cash on hand to pay the light bill.

The young man I bought the furnace from agreed to monthly payments. But one morning he startled me by showing up at my door, looking anxious.

"Wilma, I'm so sorry about Charlie. You don't have to pay me for the furnace."

Puzzled, I invited him in for coffee and asked what he meant.

A crab boat had gone down a few days before, he said, and he thought Charlie was on it.

After reassuring him that Charlie was fine, I told him we would always appreciate his kindness and that we would certainly continue to pay for the furnace.

Three weeks later, as the young man flew with his four children from Homer to Kodiak in his small plane, it crashed into a mountainside in bad weather. The family shopping spree in Homer had left no room in the plane for his wife; she had taken a commercial flight instead.

Our lifestyle in Kodiak sometimes evoked rebellion from our usually cooperative kids. One evening, we were eating a meal of roast beef, mashed potatoes, vegetable, and dessert when teenager Carmen sighed, and laid down her fork.

"What's the matter honey?" I inquired.

Her response was quick and definite: "How long are we going to have to eat this artificial meat and sawdust potatoes?"

While I should have been angry, I realized it wasn't the meal she was complaining about—it was the taste. In all her life, Carmen had eaten commercial beef only a half-dozen times. To someone used to tender Alaska moosemeat, and the sweeter, more moist local potatoes, this meal was definitely not up to par.

For the most part, it was business as usual at the beach the third season. The whole family showed up to fish, and we all lived in the cabin again. But the season was more frustrating than usual: Saltwater and weather had taken its toll on the trucks sent to pick up our fish. Unreliable, the vehicles caused costly delays, and it was all we could do to take the situation in stride.

Jesus & The Rainbow

That winter we decided to return to Kodiak, but the town was not doing well. Crabbing was down and the economy was in a slump. So Charlie went fishing on the *Loretta-O* for Dungeness crab.

Even in hard times, it was always fun when Charlie came home because he brought goodies. Sometimes it was an unlucky halibut that had ventured into a crabpot, or clams or crab. One time, after helping a man with boat trouble, the crew was rewarded with a hindquarter of elk.

By then, the trailer was paid off, and we decided to sell it and move to nearby Woody Island. While packing, I came across four-year-old David's huge, tattered stuffed cat.

"Get rid of that thing," I said, tossing it over to him.

I never asked what he did with it, but he must have thrown it in the water. Because when we pulled up to the dock on Woody Island, there, tilted up against a piling, sat that tattered, bedraggled—and now waterlogged—cat. I guess even the stuffed ones have nine lives!

We all enjoyed the time we spent on Woody Island and its acres of wild cranberries and big population of rabbits. I was pregnant and unemployed, and there wasn't much work for Charlie. With our income dropping to about $30 per week, all those berries and bunnies soon became the mainstay of our diet.

After our move to the island, Terrill, 11, quickly made friends with the local kids. One evening, a bunch of them came over in a car to pick him up. Glad about the friends, but concerned about what they were up to, I asked:

"Terrill, what on earth do you kids find to do in the dark?"

"Oh, we have a lot of fun, Mom. We go on rat patrol."

"Now, how do you do that?"

"We go to the dump in the car, then two of us get out and sit on the fenders with .22 rifles. With the lights off, we drive quickly into the dump, turn the lights on, and see who can shoot the most rats."

I pondered that for a minute, remembering my few encounters with the elusive little beasts.

"Does anyone actually hit a rat under those conditions?"

"Sometimes," he said grinning. "But we really need a shotgun and nobody will let us use one."

To a mother, that was truly a comforting thought.

Getting into the spirit of island life, little David made it his special duty to wave good-bye to every passing crab boat. Sometimes, the fishermen would respond with a toot of the horn, and this excited David so much, he'd run into the house shouting: "Mama, Mama, they honked at me."

When he wasn't waving at boats, David kept busy coloring or asking me questions. One day, he approached me, looking very serious:

"Mom, where do babies come from, anyway?"

Being from the old school, my answer was ready-made.

"Oh, they slide down the rainbow when Jesus gets ready to send them to earth."

I thought we were both happy with that answer, but one day, David came running into the house on the verge of crying:

"Mama! You have to do something quick or something awful is going to happen!" Anxiously, he pulled on my hand as we ran together out the back door.

Above us, the sky was filled with a bright, beautiful rainbow. I stared at it, trying to figure out what the problem was.

"Mom, look! The end of the rainbow is over the water. If Jesus sends a baby down now, it'll get drowned."

"Oh honey," I said, taking him in my arms. "Jesus never loads the rainbow without checking to see where the end is first."

Sighing, David smiled.

Whew! Emergency over.

Making Improvements

In the winter of 1967, Charlie made a deal on a 28-foot fishing boat, the *Sand Piper*. It didn't look like much, but with his efforts and every dime we could scrape up, it was seaworthy and beautiful for its voyage to Bristol Bay the following spring.

For the first leg of its 250-mile journey from Homer—the 70-mile distance across Cook Inlet—the boat was towed by a friend, Alex Flyum.

In Iliamna Bay, Charlie's dad met him with a truck and a lowboy trailer for the portage crossing to Lake Iliamna. This was home country to Charlie, and a trip he had made many times. But this was the first time he had traveled it as a customer.

By that time, the kids and I were already on the beach, so Charlie hurried the *Sand Piper* down the 100-mile length of Lake Iliamna and into the Kvichak River, and headed out to Bristol Bay and Naknek to fuel up for the journey to the beach.

Knowing that Charlie might arrive in Naknek that day, I flew in for groceries. It was low tide, and all the boats lay anchored on the south side of the river's main channel. I had no trouble finding the *Sand Piper* because of the big skiff we called *Old Yaller* hanging off the stern, loaded to the gunwales with supplies and building materials.

A few hours later, when the tide came in, I found a ride across the river. Boarding the *Sand Piper,* I was welcomed by a sleepy Charlie.

At daylight, Charlie inched the boat cautiously out of the Naknek River. When we neared our sites, the kids saw us coming. They jumped up and down with excitement as we pulled close to shore and anchored up.

After waving hello, my first thought was to get the supplies on shore; Charlie's was to get his new drift boat to the fishing grounds. Everyone helped off-load, and the minute we took the last item from the deck,

Charlie pulled anchor and was gone, laying a "rooster tail" wake behind him.

By then, we were set for fishing, and had the added advantage of a truck barged in on the *Tootsie*. We also moved out of the cabin, and into our 30-man squad tent. Although the tent was roomy, it was cold and whispered in the wind, constantly causing frayed nerves. Although we built a frame and floor for it, when a bad wind arose, we thought it might go airborne. On those nights, Charlie and Mike tied the tent frame to the truck; even a Bristol Bay wind couldn't take 6,500 pounds of army truck off the ground!

As we shivered through the summer, it became increasingly obvious we needed a house with windows and a proper stove. Cooking for 11 people on two camp stove burners was a real test of ingenuity. I thought a lot about that during that summer; hoping for a season good enough that we could put these things on next year's wish list.

Pedal To The Metal

The winter of 1968 passed quickly, and we remained financially solvent. Charlie was off fishing a lot, but it was what he loved to do. It was already time to plan for our next Bristol Bay season, now an established pattern, and we were learning the ropes.

For the new season, a chartered plane picked us up in Kodiak and took us directly to the beach. On the way, we flew over Shelikof Straits, down Becharof Lake, past smoking Mount Peulik, and down the Egegik River right to our doorstep. The scenery was magnificent, and the convenience of landing right on the beach without changing planes in King Salmon was outstanding. There was just one ominous note; it was predicted to be a very bad fishing season.

Still in Kodiak, Charlie ran a loader on a construction job. That season, we decided he should stay put in case the fishing was as bad as predicted. It was great logic, but when he took us to the plane, I looked sadly at him as I flew away with the kids.

While we were in Kodiak, our belongings were stored at Coffee Point, five miles away from our sites. When the girls, Terrill, David and I arrived, we found that our truck had a flat tire.

We attacked the problem with vigor, wanting to get to the beach before evening. Using the propane torch, we heated the lug nuts enough to break them loose. With tire irons, we broke the tire from the rim and removed the inner tube. Down by the Egegik River, we pumped a little air into it, pushed it underwater, and searched for bubbles, which came only from the valve stem. All of that work had been unnecessary! I replaced the valve core and we remounted the tire.

The tire in place, Coni and I climbed into the front seat with the little ones. Everybody else climbed on the back of the truck and on top of our belongings.

Glad to be underway, I eased the heavily loaded truck toward a steep grade and down a 50-foot bank. Gently, I pressed the brake as we crested the hill and picked up speed on the way down. Suddenly, it flashed in my mind—we had no brakes! (This was not unusual at the bay; brakes seldom survived the saltwater and sand more than a couple of years.) My heart turned over, as I reminded myself to stay calm.

"Coni, holler at the kids to hang on tight."

Already in low gear, I shut off the key. I felt a lot better after we turned and headed up the beach. As we approached Bishop Creek, the truck came to a stop. I got out and surveyed the spot where I wanted to cross. Because of the ever-changing sands, Bishop Creek was a place where you could easily bog down a truck.

Climbing back in, I backed up a little, started rolling, shifted to low, and poured on the juice. As I hit the gas, the kids, flapping in the breeze, hung onto the ropes topside. Laughing as we splashed through the water, we climbed the opposite bank, and went chugging along the beach.

Bishop Creek

Pulling close to our campsite about four in the afternoon, we were greeted by the sight of our collapsed tent frame. Night was coming, the frame had to be rebuilt, and the kids were hungry. Somehow, I had to find the tools I needed in the loaded truckbed.

Unloading the truck, we located the sleeping bags and readied a place on the tent floor to put our little ones. As Coni fixed some food, I took a deep breath, looked at the pile of 2-by-4s, and thought:

Well, Wilma, if you've got it to do—get on with it!

Battleship Gray

We had a great fishing season, and by winter we were back in Kodiak making plans for a new cabin at the beach. We haunted the Navy surplus yard for helpful items, buying up five dollar buckets of paint. The color wasn't great, but it was good enough for the Navy! We also got a huge roll of tough building paper with a tarry substance sandwiched in the middle.

That spring, we went to the bay early to begin the cabin. It was Charlie's first major building project and he was a nervous wreck. Finally, I said: "Honey, we won't be entertaining the President that I know of. Do your best and stop worrying over 1/64th of an inch!"

Mike and Charlie cut boards and pounded nails. When the framing was done, we wrapped it in that wonderful Navy-surplus building paper, floor and all, and we never had a draft in that little 16-by-24 structure. As Mike and Charlie nailed up the plywood siding, the kids and I—armed with paint, rollers and brushes—painted every facet of it. A week went by, and there she stood in all her battleship gray glory. We were so proud of it, especially Charlie. Twenty years later, it still looked good!

Although we nursed a few blisters from our painting and hammering experiences, we were all happy to move into our new house. I now had a kitchen with a sink, a propane stove with a real oven, a gas washing machine, and a table big enough for everyone to sit down together. From my wonderful kitchen, I loved watching the wildlife behind the house—caribou grazing on the hillside, sandhill cranes flying around their nesting area, and in the lake, the huge white swans teaching their little ones how to swim.

Meanwhile, my little ones were growing up. They were becoming more independent and had more interests of their own. But still, we fished together. And as a family, we loved our life at the bay.

Shortly after acquiring our first CB radio, our family had a pleasant surprise. I was busy in the kitchen, when suddenly the radio blared forth:

"This is Snake Eyes, Snake Eyes. I'll be on the beach at Big Creek in five minutes with fresh fruit, vegetables, meat and ice cream."

We hadn't had any of those things since spring, and it certainly sounded good. About that time, I heard the familiar sound of an Otter engine. Everyone else must have heard it, too, because up and down the beach people emerged from their setnet cabins, all jumping into their fish-hauling trucks in search of Snake Eyes.

Quickly, I found my purse and joined the parade down the beach. By the time I arrived, Snake Eyes (I never knew his real name), had loaded up a folding table with bright red tomatoes, fresh orange carrots, and luscious melons and grapes. Nearby, coolers held frozen goodies like ice cream, steaks and pork chops.

At first, the prices were a shock (I was lucky to bring home change from $100), but the quality of the goods was excellent, and my family's pleasure soothed any of my misgivings.

Navigational Hazard

Setnetting has its own particular set of problems _ like when the truck picking up the fish is late, a big tide is coming up fast, and the hundreds of fish you've just caught are about to float away. On more than one occasion we had to string them on the running line to save them—and believe me, stringing fish is not like stringing beads, especially when it is wet and cold.

In a situation like this, our truck was a convenience that we did not take for granted. With four muddy fish in each hand, we would dash up the beach, toss them in the back of the truck, and go back for more. The sand on the beach was packed well enough that the airplanes could land on it, so if we were careful the trucks could maneuver the beach too.

The truck was our life line, and for that reason, it was important that the kids learn to drive as early as possible. By the time the kids were six they were sitting on my lap and steering. By the time they were ten, sitting on a pillow with one behind them they could learn to shift gears while I still handled the clutch and brake. By that time they were familiar with checking the oil, changing oil, using a jack, and replace a tire in ten minutes.

At sixteen when the law allows kids to drive' my kids were ready to go and most of the time it worked great but one time it backfired.

On a dark rainy night in mid July, A stiff breeze was blowing, and a fierce surf pounded as the tide worked its way shoreward. We were picking fish like crazy, pushing hard to finish before we had to deal with the tide. Usually it was Tommy who would finish picking first and get the truck and start loading fish but that night when I heard the truck start I looked over and Tommy was still at work picking fish. After a while when no truck showed up to start loading fish, I began to worry a bit and I dare not leave my net to go see. I had just cleared my net and started down the beach to check when Terrill fourteen came running up to me.

"Mom, I think I lost the truck."

Now those are action words on the beach. It may seem impossible for a 44 year old woman, dressed in hip boots and slicker who had just picked 700 fish at two in the morning to run. But truth was I ran like a gazelle. One look at the truck with water up to the running boards and I knew he was right. He had taken the truck too far down the beach and tried too hard to get it out before coming for help.

Claire came by with the Michigan loader. Up to our arm pits in the pounding advancing surf we hooked on to the truck but it was so buried that the cable snapped immediately

In the end the tide came crashing in on us, washing hundreds of fish out of the truck bed and hundreds from our other nets away and covering the truck.

At dawn Charlie came home from drift netting. I was sitting at the table with a cup of tea trying to think where to start on the problem. His first question, of course, was

"Where is the truck?"

"Well dear, it is now a navigational hazard. You are lucky you did not hit when you came in across the top of it."

At other times he might have gotten mad at me but perhaps my red eyes and beaten look told him this was not the time.

As soon as the tide receded we lashed empty gas drums together, attached them to the truck and anchored it all to the beach. The bad news was that it did not work. We had to get several pieces of equipment to once again get the truck parked by the house.

Terrill never found it easy to say "I am sorry" but in his own way he said it. He took every sandy piece of that truck apart, dried it in my oven and put it back together. With a few new electrical parts it ran again. And he was forgiven and we were proud of his mechanical ability.

Full Speed For The Beach

When the weather was good, Charlie anchored the *Sand Piper* in front of the cabin. This saved him the mile-long walk from Clair's Big Creek camp, a more protected mooring.

One evening Charlie's fishing partner, his youngest brother Raymond, was playing Monopoly with the kids in our cabin. When it was time to sleep, Raymond wasn't ready to go to the boat, and we didn't have an extra bed for him.

"That's no problem," I told him. "I'll just stay out with Charlie and you can have my bed. I'll come ashore when it's time to go fishing."

A done deal, I grabbed my nightie and followed Charlie to the boat.

Sometime in the night, I sensed danger, and awakened enough to climb out of my bunk to see what was going on. At first, all I could see from the wheelhouse window was a wall of green water. Rubbing my eyes, I looked again. The wall was gone, but the boat rose to what seemed like the top of the world. From there, I could see miles of giant waves.

It was time to wake Charlie.

"Honey, wake up. We're in an awful storm."

Pulling on his jeans, Charlie lit a cigarette, picked up a tide book, and stepped out on the deck to read it. Just then, more green water whisked past the wheelhouse and put out his cigarette.

Scared to death, I waited to see what he would do. Finishing his second smoke, he looked at his watch, started the engine, and said to me:

"Wil, take the wheel. Steer straight ahead into the wind while I pull the anchor."

I was horrified and protested. "Charlie—I'm not a boat person—I don't know what I'm doing!"

Kindly, Charlie didn't remind me that I was the only help he had. Paying little attention to my objection, he vacated the wheelhouse, leaving me alone to steer the boat. Surprisingly, it went well. And when he was safely back in the wheelhouse, I asked carefully:

"Charlie, what are we going to do?" I used the term "we" loosely because all I could do was stand there shaking.

"In a few minutes, I am going to put the boat on the beach," he said.

I didn't want to second-guess him—but was that the right thing to do? I had seen movies where people survived horrible storms at sea only to perish in the churning surf.

But this was Charlie's world, and I had to trust his judgment. But just in case, I pulled on my jeans and shirt and grabbed my jacket—if I drowned, I didn't want to be a naked corpse.

Soon, another mountainous green wave rose before us. As we gained the crest, Charlie spun the little *Sand Piper* around, and we surfed full speed for the beach.

Thinking I might be approaching the last minutes of my life, I pondered whether to jump off the boat at the first feel of sand, or go down in the final splash with Charlie. Taking a firm grip on the back of his slicker, I made my decision: "Whither thou goest, I go, Charlie George."

The beach was coming up fast, and at the last possible second, Charlie spun the wheel hard to starboard. As the wave retreated back out to sea, the *Piper* laid over on its portside, tipped toward shore.

Stepping off the boat, Charlie reached for my hand to help me down. As we walked up the beach, our arms around each other, I realized it was good that Charlie was holding onto me. With all the shaking my knees were doing, I didn't think I could have made it on my own.

The Bloodcurdling Scream

It was late November, and the house we were renting on Woody Island needed some roof patching. As Charlie and Mike climbed the steep roof, I worried about them falling.

"Honey," I said to Charlie. Why don't you hook a safety line to the pickup and toss it over the house?" The men laughed like I was the worrywart of all time.

Ten minutes later, I heard a bloodcurdling scream. As I ran outside, Charlie was hopping toward the house. He had fallen off the roof, landed cockeyed on a piece of wood, and turned his ankle.

Pulling his shoe off, we could see that the foot was already swollen and turning purple. I called Chet Webber, Charlie's fishing partner in Kodiak, and asked him to bring the *Loretta-O* over as quick as possible.

As luck would have it, sea conditions were lousy, there was a blowing snow, and the boat ramp was iced up. Since Charlie weighed over two hundred pounds, I wondered how we would ever manage to get him aboard.

I shouldn't have worried. Even on one foot, Charlie was a natural-born boat person. He hopped down that icy ramp, took a deep breath, and jumped from the float to the bobbing boat without any problem.

In Kodiak, the doctor determined that the ankle was cracked, but not broken. Even so, it was terribly painful. That night, we decided not to return to the island. Instead, we stayed on a bed of sofa cushions on a friend's living room floor.

Toward morning, as Charlie tossed and turned in pain, he stuck his foot out from under the covers to see if his toes still worked. From the end of a table, the big white family cat (whose territory we were occupying), studied the situation; it was too much to resist. Full force, he pounced on Charlie's damaged foot, and the howl Charlie let out was truly phenomenal.

From a sound sleep, I jumped to my feet, trying to figure out what was happening. One look at the cat, and Charlie holding his foot, told the story; I couldn't help but laugh. It is a wonder that Charlie didn't kill me for that; it wasn't until MUCH later that he, too, could enjoy the humor of it.

Around Christmas, we heard that some cannery work had come up in Homer. We all hated to leave Woody Island, but in those days, we had to go where the work was.

On New Year's Day 1969, when we boarded the *Tustumena* ferry, I was six months pregnant. It was a delight when, in early April, our son Brad was born. He didn't seem as healthy as the other children, but with the older children not at home, I had more time to rock him and play with him.

Little did I know this was the calm before the storm.

Sobering News

The next fishing season was a blur. Our new son, Brad, picked up a bug from the water at the bay. After seeing the health nurse in Naknek and the cannery doctor, he was still not improving.

Before I left the bay, Charlie and I discussed moving to Ketchikan where a new airport was being built. Once there, my priority would be to take Brad to see Dr. Wilson, a physician recommended to us, and Charlie would try to get a job.

The kids and I arrived Saturday morning before Charlie. I rented a hotel room and immediately took Brad to the doctor's office. When I reached it, the door was locked, and turning away, I started to cry.

Just then, the door opened and a little gray-haired nurse spoke softly to me:

"What is it, dear?"

I explained the situation as she steered us into the office. Soon, Dr. Wilson appeared and took my baby from my arms. That little darling, as sick as he was, managed to look up at the doctor and give him a tired little smile.

But the doctor's attention was not on Brad.

"How long has it been since you've slept?" he asked me.

"I can't remember," I answered, trying to control the sobs.

"I want you to take this little child to the hospital, get him checked in, and go home and sleep. We will take good care of him there."

I was too tired to protest. Following the doctor's instructions, I slipped into a troubled sleep, and at 4 a.m., I woke up scared to death that Brad needed me. I raced to the hospital, and there he was in an oxygen tent with an I.V. in his arm—sleeping peacefully. I collapsed into a nearby rocking chair, and slept again. The nurse sent me home, but very shortly the doctor called me back.

Dr. Wilson was very direct. "Mrs. Williams, I am afraid that Brad has Cystic Fibrosis; he seems to have enough of the symptoms to confirm the diagnosis."

"Doctor, I don't know anything about that disease. What are you telling me?"

"Well, Cystic Fibrosis impairs the body's ability to fight disease. If Brad had all the symptoms—which he doesn't—he would be lucky to see his 12th birthday."

To the doctor, my reaction may have looked something like the calm I usually mustered in the face of disaster. But actually, something else guided me: The unshakable belief that I would never lose any of my children.

The doctor continued.

"As it is, I am going to prescribe a series of gamma globulin shots and, if things go well, he just might grow out of it by the time he's five."

I was grateful that he was so straightforward, but this was very sobering news.

We stayed in Ketchikan for the winter, coping with Brad's painful shots, and as always, looking forward to our next season at the bay.

The Red Beard

The following season, Charlie flew into Naknek early to help with construction of the Whitney Fidalgo cannery building. When I arrived with Brad, I couldn't believe how much my husband had changed: He had grown the reddest full beard I had ever seen. As Charlie went to hug us, I wondered if the beard would scare the baby. But instead, Brad put his little arms up to his father and cooed, "My Daddy."

Things were looking up. Brad was just over one year old, doing well, gaining weight, and beginning to get a little color. Dr. Wilson felt that he could go through the summer without any shots. That was great news to us and we all kept our fingers crossed—but it was not the end of our family's medical woes.

During the season, seven-year-old David fell off the truck and a tire ran over his leg. Everything happened so fast, I didn't get the full story until we were airborne in a medevac plane.

"How did this happen?" I asked him, expecting him to talk about his broken leg.

"I'm sorry, Mom. I tried to keep my head away from the truck, but the tire ran me over anyway."

His voice shook as he relived the incident in his mind.

He must be hysterical, I thought, *it was his leg he injured—not his head.* But just to be sure he didn't have two injuries, I looked closer. It was then I noticed three red marks where a tire had scraped against his face.

A little later, Terrill, too, was injured when he jumped into the hold of a boat. His coveralls got caught on a moving propeller shaft, wrapping his leg around it. The injury gangrened, and his leg was amputated from the knee down.

"It's really bad," Coni told me when it happened, and she was right.

As risky and changeable as it was, the bay had become the constant in our lives. Sometimes it was calm and serene, the white, restless clouds scudding across an azure sky. When it was like that, the water's silky surface mirrored the fishing boats at anchor, and it was a beautiful sight to see.

At other times, the bay was vastly different. Angry, frothing waves attacked the shoreline with a vengeance, as though to punish it for existing. Swirling, shifting sands hurried before an excited wind, stinging our faces and eyes, seeking to invade every fold of our clothing.

As the seasons progressed, none of this ever changed my enduring love for the place.

Possession Next Spring

In 1972, Charlie came home to the beach from working at the cannery in Naknek and I had been fishing for several weeks. He went visiting the neighbors, and returned with some interesting news:

"Did you know Dean Wallace wants to sell Coffee Point?"

Coffee Point sat at the mouth of the Egegik River, five miles south of our fishing sites.

"What does he want for it?" I asked.

"I don't know. When do we eat?"

As we finished dinner, I thought more about Coffee Point. The following day I made a request: "Charlie, I'm tired of being in the house. How about taking me out for a ride?"

"Where do you want to go?" he answered agreeably, reaching for his jacket.

"Why don't we go and see Dean? I haven't been to Coffee Point at all this year."

As fate would have it, Dean was home, and offered us something to drink. After visiting for a while, I said:

"Dean—Is it true you want to sell out here at the Point?"

"Yes. I've been thinking about it."

"How much did you have in mind?"

He gave me a price and told me what was included.

Shocking Charlie, I asked Dean if he would take $1,000 down, another payment at the end of the season, and the balance on terms.

I would have gone a bit slower, but I felt it was important to our future to own land we could have title to, unlike the place we were living.

I made out a check on the spot. And then I said: "Dean, we should write this down on something so we won't forget or have any misunderstandings later."

He agreed, but neither of us could find a piece of paper. Finally, I took out my pack of cigarettes, emptied the sticks into my pocket, opened the package flat, and wrote down the terms for the five-acre homesite. At the end I added "possession next spring," and we all three signed it. For years, that was the only paperwork we had on Coffee Point.

One time, when the fishing was bad, I wondered how we could feed the kids and still pay Dean. Without prompting, Dean stopped by for a cup of coffee, and said to me: "Wilma—Do you think you could pay just the interest this fall? Maybe next year, if the fishing's better, you can pay a little extra to make up the difference."

How simple life was in those days. And what a wonderful friend we had in Dean.

During our last season at the other end of the beach, the summer of 1972, I spent extra time enjoying our wildlife neighbors—the caribou, swans, muskrats and sandhill cranes. The prospect of moving to Coffee Point was exciting, but to do it, I had to abandon our beloved battleship gray cabin and work new fishing sites. I would miss all the wonderful times we shared together, and the way we painted our way out of the cabin each fall, so that it would be fresh and ready for us to return to in the spring. The older kids would continue to use the house, but I knew it was the end of an era for us.

PART TWO

COFFEE POINT

The Move

We were now the owners of a five-acre homesite, a big house, an array of cabins and vehicles, two boats, and new fishing sites. This was progress, but it was with mixed feelings that I packed the things in the gray house by the lake. Each room of the cabin was wrapped in its own memories, and each one tugged at my heartstrings. It reminded me of how my children were growing up, and I started suffering the feelings mothers get when they see their nests emptying. But I wasn't there yet—Brad was only three years old and I still had a few years of in-house mothering left to do!

As the last box was taped shut, I dutifully climbed into the truck beside Charlie. As we rolled toward our new home, we passed through Bishop Creek, across the few miles of hard-packed sand, and made the final turn to Coffee Point.

Once we were settled in, we learned that we had to do some things differently. Instead of peeking out the front door to see if the tide was right to pick our nets, we had to drive two miles up the beach to our new sites. The trucks we inherited from Dean were old. We made a habit of traveling the high beach so they would not be swamped by the tides if they quit running on us.

For drinking, we hauled water from a spring that flowed just around the Point; it was the best water I'd ever had. We had a well with a hand pump closer to the house, but before we could use it, we had to do some extensive cleaning. Even at the bay, little creatures like mice have a tendency to fall into wells, as we discovered when we opened it up. After we purified it, the water ran clear.

Mel's Story

We hadn't been at the point long before our neighbor, Mel Ackley, came up from Washington and began to visit us on a regular basis. He owned two of the cabins that sat on our land, and liked to come over for coffee and conversation.

"Are you folks going to fall-fish for silvers?" he asked one morning late in the summer.

"Yes, we really enjoy the fishing when things quiet down a little."

"I'd sure like to stay around for it, but I miss my family. I'm going to write my wife Doris about bringing the kids up for a couple of weeks."

"It'd be nice to meet them," we agreed.

Later in the morning, I went down to Red and Margaret's to process fish and found Mel hard at work, doing the same.

"Are you going out fishing today?" I asked. "It's looking a little sloppy out there."

"You bet I'm going—I can't let that Charlie get too far ahead of me!" he said good-naturedly, taking off his apron and walking toward the beach.

After finishing up at Red and Margaret's, I went home to do my baking, occasionally glancing out the window as I always did. I saw Mel coming.

At one point, I watched Mel try to tie his skiff to a buoy about 50 feet offshore and miss. Circling around, he came back for another try and seemed to have a hold. Just then, I turned away to scoot the coffee pot to the hotter part of the stove.

I was called back to the window by what sounded like a terrible scream. By that time, Charlie was on the beach with his deckhand, David Alto, yelling to me.

"Wil, come here—hurry! Mel's under the water!"

He had come around the Point just in time to see Mel fly out of the skiff, his line wrapped fatally around one foot.

"I'm going for help," I hollered, running as fast as I could the half-mile to Red and Margaret's.

When I got back, Mel's lifeless body lay on the beach. The tide and current had stripped away all the clothes from his upper body. We did CPR for an hour, but it was hopeless.

Our friend was gone.

When they asked me for information to notify his wife, I let myself into Mel's house. Sitting on the table, I found the letter he had written earlier in the morning asking her to come up.

Later, I wrote to her and included the letter so she would know his last thoughts were of her and the family.

New Beginnings

Just before we moved to Coffee Point, Tommy turned 22 and was working in Seattle. One day the phone rang, and it was TomTom saying:

"Mom, I feel like quitting my job and coming back to Alaska."

He'd been with his company a long time, and I knew he wouldn't quit lightly. But I'd had inklings of his unhappiness once when he called me from work. In the background I heard someone yell at him:

"Get busy there!"

I couldn't believe it when my independent son Tommy answered, "Yes, sir!"

I didn't say anything at the time, but I wanted to shout: "Run, Tom, run."

Now he was on the phone asking me if I thought coming back to Alaska was a good idea.

"There isn't much winter work up here, son."

"I know, Mom."

"You've been with that company for three years."

"I know."

"The bottom line is: Will it make you feel better about yourself and bring you more happiness?"

"Hang up, Mom. I'll be home next week."

We both laughed and I said: "I'm so glad, honey."

And so, Tommy came back to Alaska. Luckily, it was during the famous pipeline years, and he quickly got a job driving a truck for an oil company.

Once back in Alaska, Tommy came to the beach every year to help us.

It was 1973, and so many things had changed since we started fishing Bristol Bay. Coni, now 24, returned faithfully every season with Mike to fish our old sites. Carmen, 21, now married and pregnant, was working toward her nursing credentials in California. We missed her enthusiasm and sense of humor at the beach.

After recovering from his leg injury, Terrill, 18, went to diesel school and found work on the pipeline. Tammy, 19, lived in Chestertown, Maryland with her husband and their baby Karl. After skipping a few seasons, her family got back into spending summers at the bay, living and working at the old sites.

David, 10, was still a little guy, but he was driving the pickup on the beach and picking his setnet and doing fine. His attitude toward school was a little sketchy, but at the last minute, he would always manage to pass one more grade.

Little Brad, at 4, was feeling well and already knew how to pick fish—with help. But his favorite activity was riding on the back of the three-wheeler driven by David. One day, David showed Brad how the vehicle worked, and Brad caught on faster than anyone expected.

Boy, did he go!—Through the yard, over the burm, down the beach—with all of us running frantically after him, and his dad catching him just as he was about to drive into the river.

Never a dull moment at the beach.

Wilma, David, Charlie & Brad

The Race Was On

The next spring, just before it was time to apply for our fishing licenses, we heard that the bay would not open for fishing. This was devastating news, and I wrote a letter to Fish & Game, asking if it was true. The answer came back: "In the best interests of the preservation of the fishery, the bay will not open this year."

When the April 15th deadline came up, we let it pass without registering. If we couldn't fish, what was the point of paying the fees?

Instead, we came up with other plans. Charlie made arrangements to fish Cook Inlet with our friend, Ralph Galliano. Coni went to work in a restaurant, and I opened a little gift shop on the Homer Spit.

On July 4th, the phone rang in my shop. It was a girlfriend at Bristol Bay.

"Wilma, there are fish everywhere! They're going to open it tomorrow at 1 p.m. You have got to come quick!"

I was stunned. How could we go? We weren't even registered! Soon, a second call came in from one of the companies we sold fish to, saying: "Wilma, get out here!"

I wanted to cry, thinking how I had been misled. That night I couldn't sleep, and by 4 a.m., I was fighting mad. At 9 a.m., I called the Governor's office and asked to speak to him. Instead, they connected me to the person in charge of fishery problems.

"This is Wilma Williams," I told the man. "I have a letter in my possession from the head of your Fish & Game department saying there will be no openings in the Egegik area this summer. On that basis, I didn't register. In four hours, you are opening that area, and I want you to know I will be fishing! Before I go to the site, I will stop in King Salmon for the paperwork you will prepare to allow me to fish—got that?"

"Well, ah, Mrs. Williams—we'll have to get back to you.

"Oh, that will be fine, sir—anytime in the next five minutes—I have a plane to catch."

In all honesty I didn't feel as confident as I tried to sound.

Five minutes later, as I gathered some belongings together, they called me back and agreed to my requests.

The race was on.

First, I arranged for Brad to stay with a friend, and for another friend to cover the shop. I called Homer Air to charter a flight to the bay, packed duffels for Charlie and me, asked David to pack his own, and called Coni to tell her what was happening. And lastly, when I stopped at the gas station to pick up a truck battery to take with me, I ran into Charlie.

"Grab that battery, Honey, while I make out a check, would you? The airplane is waiting."

Charlie hesitated. "Wilma, I can't go," he said. But I had no time for explanations. Instead, I tossed him his duffel bag, waved, and said: "See you later. I'm outta here! I'll leave the car at the airport with the keys in the ashtray."

Eleven-year-old David, my travel companion, was the only one too young to defend himself against my enthusiasm.

As the plane flew westward, I felt like chewing my fingernails; nothing was moving fast enough for me. We made the King Salmon stop, grabbed the paperwork and a few groceries.

By the time we got to Coffee Point, the few people who had bought their licenses had already set their nets. The pilot, Larry, did a flyover so I could see what was going on, but all I wanted was to land and set my nets. As he banked the plane for a better view, giving a running narration of what he was seeing, I groaned, put my hands over my eyes, and shouted: "Larry, shut up and land this thing!"

He laughed.

That was a wild day. After we landed, everyone was too busy fishing to give us a ride to the sites. Instead, we lugged our duffel bags, groceries and the battery up the beach. We threw our things in the house and went down to the Jeep. I turned the engine over so many times trying to start it, I ran the new battery down. The real problem, we discovered, was that a slow leak over the winter had emptied the tank of gas. I carried the ailing battery to the Clark's to get it charged. Red Clark, who had been at the beach since Day One, took one look at me and said:

"Wilma, take my truck and get your gear out!"

There are just no words to say how grateful I was.

David and I drove to the house at Coffee Point, gathered nets, running line, and buoys and—since we were both too short to drive stakes—anchors.

There was a lot of mud at the sites and by the time we got the anchor set, tied it to the buoy barrel and block, dragged the 600 feet of running line into place and attached the net, we were exhausted.

We hurried back to Red's to return his truck. That accomplished, we drove home, ate sandwiches and fell across our beds, taking time only to kick off our muddy boots.

By 4 o'clock in the morning, we were back on the beach. Our hearts sank when we saw that the anchors hadn't held. We picked the fish from the net (about 750), reset it, and before long had another 750 fish. The fisherman side of me wished for more, but my tired body didn't mind at all.

Margaret & Red Clark

Next time we set the anchors, we dug holes and buried them. Then we reset the net and went to deliver fish. David was awfully tired, and fell asleep in the truck as I unloaded our catch.

The next tide, we followed the same routine on about three hours sleep. We made it through, but were both so shaky, I couldn't hold a cup of tea.

The next day, I told David to rest, while I tried to get a message out for help.

"Okay," he said in a tired little voice, and headed straight for bed.

I tried to get a plane to take me across the river to a telephone. The pilots were sympathetic, but were tied up hauling fish.

Finally I resorted to begging.

"Just get me across, I'll find a way back," I pleaded.

"Okay," one pilot answered. "But then you're on your own."

"Right."

Once on the Egegik side of the river, I ran for the telephone to call Charlie, but he wasn't home. I reached Coni, and asked her to relay this message:

"Send help NOW! It's worth $1,000 for eight days of Tommy's or David Alto's time."

I ran to the beach, where a couple of guys were getting into a skiff. "Could I get a ride across the river with you?" I asked hopefully.

"Sure, hop in," they responded.

Lucky me!

In minutes, I was on the other side, and only about a mile from home. I woke my son David, we had soup and more sandwiches, and started down the beach again.

This time, the net held longer, and we had 1,200 fish. David was so tired, poor baby, that he whimpered all the time, but to his credit, he kept carrying fish.

I tried hard to keep up the pace, but I was moving slower and slower. Hugging David, I realized I had never been so tired in my life. As we worked, I prayed that my message to Coni would bear fruit. There was no way we could hold out much longer.

By 5 o'clock the next morning, we had slept only seven hours since arriving at the beach. Overhead, planes zoomed by hauling huge loads of fish. It was an exciting time, but it was hard to keep up but we were picking fish.

Stopping for a moment, I stood up to straighten my aching back. Glancing down the beach, I saw a figure jogging toward me. Rubbing my eyes, I looked again. There—big as life—was my TomTom.

I cried out to David, and we both ran to meet him. Between desperate hugs, Tommy looked at us, grinned, and jumped into the truck, saying:

"I'll deliver this load while you finish picking, and I'll be back with the sledgehammer and stakes shortly."

When he returned, we all loaded the rest of the fish onto the truck, and Tommy said: "That's enough work for you two. I don't need help unloading or driving stakes." Then, pointing to the house, he added: "Rest!"

What a wonderful thought.

By the end of the week, with Tommy's help, David and I had earned over $10,000. We teased Charlie, who had earned only $640 on Cook Inlet. But keeping his commitment to fish with his friend Ralph was important to him, and when he was finished there, Charlie flew to the beach and helped finish up a really fine season.

A More Stable Future

We bought a lot in Homer in the fall of 1975 and moved a trailer on it. I was delighted to find rhubarb and raspberries growing nearby, and with a little TLC, they were soon up to par.

Now that we owned land both in Homer and Coffee Point, our lives took on a more stable quality and we felt like we had a future. We were doing well enough that Charlie and I planned a March trip to Hawaii. We had never taken a real vacation, even a short one, and we were excited about going.

When Beluga Lake froze over, the Homer Hotrod Association started their winter ice racing activities. Charlie was flagman, and I ran the hot dog stand. Tommy, Coni and her husband Mike all raced. For many of us, the family-oriented affair warded off a lot of cabin fever.

During one of the last events, one car hit the burm pretty hard, straightened out, hit it a second time, and over-corrected. Then it careened toward flagman Charlie full bore.

From the hot dog stand, I saw Charlie throw up one arm, get hit by the car, and go down, but not under. Thinking quickly, he somehow managed to hook his feet on the front bumper and instead of getting run over, he was dragged along the ice.

The association members prided themselves on being well-prepared and that day they did themselves proud. In minutes, Charlie was in the ambulance and on the way to Homer Hospital. The hospital looked him over, and decided to send him by medevac plane to a specialist in Anchorage.

As we flew over the lake, Charlie, who was suffering from a compound fracture of one arm, struggled to look out the window. Sinking back, he asked, "Honey, are they into the main event yet?"

I had to laugh, answering the other question on my mind instead.

"I had better cancel our reservations to Hawaii," I told Charlie. "You aren't going to feel much like having fun."

His reaction came fast.

"We're going, Wil. I can rest just as well there as here—with a lot more sun!"

Charlie was in a cast when we boarded the plane. Everyone asked how it happened, and he was at the height of his glory telling hot rod stories about Alaska.

Ham & Eggs

We started off the next season at Coffee Point with what we thought were ideal conditions. The main house, with its corrugated tin exterior, rested on pilings on the side of the hill. This allowed us to store the trucks underneath for winter. The other four cabins that came with the deal would house the summer fishing crews.

Since we'd changed locations a few years ago, we delivered our fish to a different company. Supposedly, they had arranged for a boat to process our fish during the run. Until then, we would deliver to Red and Margaret's place as usual, and not worry about it.

Everything went according to Hoyle until July 2nd when the processor boat arrived with a skipper—but NO CREW. Seeking answers, I hurried to find Jack, the company's representative, who offered no explanations except for "That's crazy!" In my naiveté, I offered to put a crew together if the company would pay my transportation to Homer.

On July 4th, I jumped on a plane, rounded up eight able-bodied workers in Homer, and flew back with them to the beach. I was relieved when they boarded the ship, and I could head back to my fishing. The company already owed us thousands of dollars; I knew we could make this work.

That season, David and I fished together with two friends from Homer, Mary Wickersham and Sharon Shears. We were a good team and it was the most pleasant fishing season I ever had. We were running about 2,000 to 3,000 fish a tide from our four fishing locations, and we had to haul continuously to keep up. The weather was one sunny day after another, and keeping the fish properly covered with wet burlap was time-consuming. While the others picked fish, I loaded, hauled, washed, and delivered everything.

One mid-July morning, I got up and as usual, looked out my window, and there sat the processor crew from Homer—complete with bags.

"What on earth happened?" I asked, stepping outside.

"The skipper unloaded us onto a barge, and left for Seattle in the middle of the night," one of them answered.

I threw my jacket on, flew down the beach in the truck, and approached Jack. He acted just as surprised as I was; I pointed out that there was a hungry group of fishermen at my door in need of breakfast.

Jack supplied me with some ham and a couple dozen eggs, and while he made flight arrangements, I fixed the crew a good meal. Although Jack said the company would still accept our fish, most of the crew didn't want to stay around to process it; they wanted to go home.

They wanted payment, too.

"No problem," Jack said to me. "I'll cut a check to you and you can pay the crew."

"That seems like an odd way to settle up," I said, but lulled into a false sense of security by three trouble-free years of fishing for the company, I agreed.

Jack gave me two checks totaling $70,000, which I deposited, and the crew flew home with checks written on my account.

A few days later, Charlie and I were in the village of Egegik doing errands, and I decided to visit the owner of the company. We knocked on his door, he started to open it, saw us, and slammed it in our faces.

Charlie and I looked at each other questioningly, and I said:

"We have some telephone calls to make."

First, I called Coni in Homer.

"Go to the bank in the morning, ask the banker if those checks I wrote are any good, and send word to me as soon you can.

The following day, a message came back by plane—but it wasn't from Coni.

"Wilma, get on this airplane now!" my Homer banker

Oh boy.

I jumped on the plane that had delivered the message, and in a couple of hours, I was sitting in the bankers office.

He confirmed my worst fears: I had written $70,000 worth of rubber checks as the check I had been given as no good. He would not have known about it if Coni would not have contacted him. The company had not made a deposit in their account since June.

I tried to think what to do. One thing in my favor was that the company check had not bounced yet. This gave me a little time. I advised everyone not to try and cash their paychecks until I could get a handle on things. By evening, I was in Seattle at the company's main office. The following morning, I approached the head honcho, but he did not want to speak to me. He finally gave up trying to dodge me when I got loose enough to say softly:

"I will talk to you! Otherwise I have been known to raise an ungodly commotion, and I would rather not do that in your place of business. Now let's go into your office."

We marched right in.

"How do you intend to remedy this little situation that you have gotten us into?"

"Now Wilma, don't you worry. You will get your money." He said with one of his best business smiles.

"But sir what you don't understand is that every time I get $70,000 worth of rubber checks, I worry a lot."

The man squirmed in his seat, but I continued.

"Now! Start pumping up my account every day with the very best amount you can—or we will both be sorry."

He must have been convinced because that is exactly what happened.

When the final deposit was made, the company said it was $10,000 and the Homer Bank said it was $18,000. There appeared to be an $8,000 mistake in my favor caused by the Federal Reserve. I went home and called the main branch of my bank in Anchorage. The lady I spoke with was very patient with me as she explained "The Federal Reserve does not make mistakes."

"Okay, that is nice to know," I answered, "but I don't want to hear from you in a month saying you were wrong." I could almost hear the lady smiling at my stupidity.

With that take care of, I hung up the phone and got on with my life.

Later we went after the company for the $60,000 worth of fish that were ours personally but never were able to collect. We were also out of the cost of the Seattle trip. Pretty rough.

That of course was not the end of the story.

In October, I got a call from the lady at the bank.

"Mrs. Williams, I am afraid there has been an error, and you have $8,000 of the bank's money."

"Is this the same $8,000 we discussed a few months ago? The one where the Federal Reserve does not make mistakes?"

"Well that is really beside the point Mrs. Williams. You will have to come in, fill out some paper work and make arrangements to repay this immediately." She said in a crisp banky voice.

But I was ready for her.

"No, I don't feel like doing that. I agree that it is not my money, but as I have planned all along, I will pay you back next summer when I have it. Oh and thanks for letting me know that the Federal Reserve is not infallible—goodbye now." And I quietly hung up the phone.

Perhaps my banker intervened on my behalf as I heard no more and we repaid the money the following summer as we had said.

Bear Necessities

When I came back from Seattle, Charlie told me he had left the bay so fast, he really hadn't closed things up properly at Coffee Point; he needed to go back.

But he didn't tell me the details until later.

After I'd called him about the checks, he put the pile of dirty dishes into a washtub in the kitchen and locked up. After he left, the smell of food escaped from the cabin, and some lucky local bears caught the scent.

To get in, they broke the window over the sink and for starters, ate five gallons of mayonnaise, chomped down 30-dozen eggs, and ate our entire spring season supply of sugar and flour. Ripping open drygood packages, they sampled rice, beans, macaroni and noodles—but didn't finish them off. Still curious, they penetrated many of the canned goods with their teeth, sucking out the contents in a way only Alaska bears can do. And finally, they licked every dish in the sink clean—and imprinted a drippy paw mark one foot down from the ceiling as a signature.

When Charlie returned and found this scene, he filed it under "Something Wilma Should Take Care of In The Spring"—and boarded it up. I had no idea what I would be facing next season.

California Sunshine

Carmen called me from her home in Barstow, California in early January 1977.

"How are you doing, Mom?"

Ordinarily, I am not a moaner, but I had just broken my left ankle on the ice, and I let her know I was not happy about it.

"Hang up, Mom. I have an idea."

I hung up and sat there, feeling sorry for myself, until Carmen called back.

"Mom, how would you folks like to come down and run the ranch for us for pay? We're about to sell it, and our foreman leaves in a week, and it has a furnished two-bedroom house. Talk to Charlie and call us back."

Two days later, we rolled southward in Terrill's 26-foot motor home. Near Haines Junction, Alaska, the defroster fan went out at 50 degrees below zero. David and I took turns rubbing the huge windshield with a salty cloth to melt the ice so Charlie could see.

Of all the things Carmen has done for us, the invitation to the ranch was the nicest. We all turned a rich mahogany color, the boys rode horseback for the first time, Charlie took a real interest in crop management, and the lack of ice meant I could enjoy the outdoors on my crutches.

In April the place sold, and we were homeward-bound to get ready for fishing.

It was a nice trip home. When we broke over a hilltop in Northern California and saw the Pacific Ocean sprawled before us in all its turquoise beauty, we all cheered and hugged each other.

An Impressive Mess

Determined to get back on our feet financially, we flew into Coffee Point once again. It was the spring of 1977.

But first, we had to deal with the bears handiwork. I am not sure what I had expected, but it was even worse: The bears had come back for seconds and they didn't come alone.

Breaking through the kitchen window and the back door, the bears opened the entire cabin and its contents to the creature world. The combination of dry goods and animal droppings from foxes, ground squirrels, shrews and—of course, bears—was the most impressive mess I had ever seen.

The door was in splinters, and the kitchen window was gone.

Needless to say, I was not happy with Charlie.

"Put our things over there," I said, in the most civil tone I could muster.

The next morning, I felt a little guilty for being so angry, so I looked again to see if I was overreacting.

Unfortunately, I was not.

It took three days, many buckets of water, and lots of shoveling before I could see the floor of the house. Repairing my attitude took a little longer—but I knew I couldn't stay angry forever.

When I was finished, with some good help from Brad & David, Coffee Point was shining clean. Charlie had chosen that time to go to Naknek on business.

That season, Charlie sold the *Sand Piper* and ordered a new skiff. When it arrived, he painted it a bright blue and named it *Blue Bird*. On the inside of the boat's small cabin door, I wrote this poem:

A Prayer

May the God of hard-working fishermen
Smile down with pleasure and with joy,
And bless with many fishes,
This humble Homer boy.

The Bluebird

A Unique Existence

One of the reasons I liked our new house at Coffee Point was that I could do things like peel potatoes while watching the boats turn upriver.

But the closeness to the river also created some unusual situations: Sometimes, in the middle of the night, I would sit straight up in bed when a motor sounded so loud I thought it was going to come right through our bedroom. At those times, I would run to my window, and there would be a big power scow with all its lights on moving slowly by the house.

One early morning, I was sitting at the kitchen table when a movement outside caught my attention. Atop the forty foot bluff behind the house stood a big, obviously agitated, moose. His heavy breathing made a steamy cloud in the cool morning air as he looked one way and then the other with a sense of urgency.

Suddenly, the animal plunged down the bank with amazing agility and charged out across the tidal flats.

Oh, my, I thought, that poor animal will get stuck in the mud or drown.

Reaching for my binoculars, I watched the moose splash his way speedily across the sloppy sand—and vanish.

Feeling sad for the moose, I set down the glasses and fixed a cup of tea. After I added some cream to the tea, I picked up the binoculars again, hoping to see some sign of him.

On the far shore, I saw a small cloud of steam rising from the panting moose, as he moved anxiously southward.

Looking back, I can see that in some ways, we lived a unique existence at the bay.

A Phase Of Life

On May 29, 1977, the first fishing boat of the season sat out front. While fishermen might have been ready for summer, the weather wasn't cooperating; it felt like snow outside.

I was 53 years old, and I just couldn't get it through my head that my body was slowing down. I'd go down to the sites, pick a few fish, and the next day I couldn't walk. I still did the baking and cooking, but I was beginning to feel crippled all the time. I was at the age, I finally realized, when you start paying for abusing your body—even if it is with honest labor. When the day came that I had to give up fishing altogether, it broke my heart. It was the end, I knew, of a phase of my life.

To make myself useful, I started answering the CB radio. People soon learned that I would be home when everyone else was out picking fish. One of the local charter companies, Pen Air, often called to ask if I would pick someone up from a flight. Sometimes I helped haul fish, but I didn't feel like I belonged anymore.

Even so, we had a good season that year. We made enough money to get caught up on our bills and pay for the *Blue Bird*.

That year we stayed around longer and fall-fished, and smoked and canned some fish to take home to Homer. With most people gone for the season, there were fewer demands on my time, so I went out fishing with Charlie. The weather was beautiful and it was nice to spend time with him.

After we returned to Homer in October, we heard that a bad storm had worked its way north from Hawaii to Alaska, devastating the western coastline.

This made us nervous, so Charlie went back to the bay to check on things.

His report was bleak—the front beach at Coffee Point was a disaster. All of the plywood, extra doors and windows stored underneath the house were either gone entirely or scattered along the beach. Angry waves had eroded the shoreline under one of our little buildings, and it was partly balanced in mid-air. Gas barrels, both empty and full, were strung for miles. And one of the cabins had washed off its foundation and lay intact, but at a rakish angle, on the beach.

Charlie salvaged what he could, but, once again, we would have a big clean-up job to do in the spring.

Ready To Party

In 1978, our goals were to get things cleaned up and make the last payments on Coffee Point.

My cousin Isabell, whom we called Ibby, came out to the Point from Oregon to help in the kitchen. Ibby is a precise person, and I think our way of life was a shock to her system. Recipe books and pre-planning are musts with her—nice, but not always possible at the bay.

One day, despite my program of slowing down, I came running into the house after hauling fish, and said:

"Hi, Ibby! We're having 12 people to lunch in half an hour."

A look of absolute horror came over her face. Slowly, shaking her head, she said: "We can't do that. There's not enough time."

"Oh sure we can," I said, dumping a box of biscuit mix into a big bowl.

"We'll have creamed tuna over hot biscuits, buttered green beans, and cole slaw. You do the slaw—both heads of cabbage—and I'll catch the rest, okay?"

Turning to the task, Ibby kept shaking her head over such goings-on, but she fixed the slaw and the meal was ready—complete with cookies and fruit for dessert—when the hungry crew pulled in for lunch.

One day in late June after 12 hours of fishing, there were only about 25 fish caught on the entire beach. Everyone worried because we should have been having pretty good picks by then.

Jumpers—salmon leaping out of the water to shake their eggs free—had been sighted on the incoming tide the evening before. This was usually a sign of good fishing to come.

As we rolled into July, Fish & Game still hadn't declared any extra openings and there was no sign of the run. On the First; no fish. On the Second; no fish and on the Third, still no fish. Tensions ran high, because most people buy their fishing supplies and nets on credit before the season. No fish means no money to pay these debts. This weighed heavily on a lot of people's minds.

To counteract all that tension, I got an idea and broadcast it over CB radio:

"Tomorrow, everybody is invited to bring a hot dish to Coffee Point for a Fourth of July Celebration. We will eat about noon, but plan to stay all afternoon."

By noon the next day, our house was filled with setnetters and a few drifters carrying potluck dishes. Charlie used a 4-by-8 sheet of plywood to make a table in the yard to enlarge the kitchen table, and I added a bed sheet as a tablecloth. Then I opened both doors of the house so that people could enter one way, fill their plates, and leave out the other.

The kids opted to provide the salmon, so down to the river they ran, squealing and shouting, spearing fish and throwing them on the riverbank. Charlie barbecued the catch, tossing on some chicken for variety, and I whipped up some potato salad as a side dish.

Loretta Chapman

The food was great, as were the sack and three-legged races. But the real highlight of the day was "The Style Show," a kind of Bristol Bay fashion show, featuring fishing gear modeled with all the luxury and flair of tuxedos and prom dresses.

The day's grand finale was the "Downtown Coffee Point Parade." Everyone jumped onto the crusty, smelly fish-hauling trucks, and Harley Hess, riding in the lead truck, got out his accordion and played songs like "Yankee Doodle Dandy," "God Bless America," and "The Star Spangled Banner," with everyone singing.

As the trucks progressed down the beach, we sang at the top of our voices and some of us waved little American flags.

Afterwards, tired and happy, everyone said good-bye to their neighbors and turned their trucks toward their home camps.

The following day, July 5, our attention turned back to fishing—or the lack of it. Some people left the beach, afraid there would be no more openings. At Coffee Point, we sent Ibby home to cut down on expenses.

The next day, as the tide started in, a few jumpers showed up. Curious, people went down to the beach, calling their friends and neighbors over the CBs. Soon, the tide was really running, and fish were everywhere—as far as the eye could see. Before or since, I have never seen so many fish in the air! Elated, we all jumped up and down and hugged each other.

But all that activity didn't mean we could fish. It was up to Fish & Game to determine that. And all that day, there was no word from them.

Finally the next day, just when the most docile among us was ready to fly to King Salmon to confront them, Fish & Game gave us an opening. It was great—the run lasted for days.

At the end of July, I made out the final check to Dean Wallace for our purchase of Coffee Point. We had reached our goal with a lot of hard work and persistence and it was a good feeling.

Before we left the bay, we moved the cabins away from the receding beach, cut a road up the hill I dubbed "Alder Way," and made plans to build a new house there the following spring.

On August 15th, when the plane came to take us home, all hands were ready and waiting. We all loved the bay, but it had been an emotional season of ups and downs. In Homer, I looked forward to making maple bars for my family and canning fish for winter, as usual.

More Than Cookies

Now that we had the title to Coffee Point, Charlie and I discussed starting a business of some kind. I suggested a cold storage plant for fish, but Charlie didn't seem interested one way or the other.

I made a few phone calls.

"Could you give me a price on a cold storage plant?" I asked.

After a moment of silence, I would get an answer like: "Did an engineer draw up your plans and specifications?"

"No," I responded.

"Well, first we would need that, then we have to do a study, and then we'd have to go over it with the engineer, and then . . ."

Wilma, you're in over your boot tops already, and you have only asked one question.

"How much does an engineer cost to do those things?"

Well, of course, there was no direct answer to that either, but the figure of $80,000 floated casually by me.

With that answer, I went back to baking chocolate chip cookies for Charlie and the boys in the kitchen, the place the cold storage people seemed to think I belonged.

In mid-October, I got a call from an old friend, Jake Jacobson, who had run a cannery in Egegik the first season we were at the bay. After chatting a bit, he asked me:

"Wilma, how would you like to build a boat storage unit at Coffee Point?"

I was quiet for a minute, then asked:

"Why would I do that?"

"Because storing one boat for one season earns about $2,000 per vessel."

That was a number I liked.

The canneries, he said, usually handled the boat storage for their fishermen. But times were changing.

"The cannery I work for wants to purchase fish at a better price from the fishermen. To do this, they have to let fishermen make their own arrangements for their boats. Coffee Point is a good location; you should consider it."

He had my attention.

"Give me a couple of days to kick it around, talk to Charlie, and I'll give you an answer."

I did some checking, drew some rough building designs, and found out more about the costs.

When I had a few answers, I approached Charlie on the subject.

"Honey, do we want to build a boat storage at the point?"

He told me he had to think about it.

The next day, he said that a friend thought it was a lousy idea, and that it was silly to think we could get the financing we needed, anyway. I wanted his personal opinion, not his friend's.

On my own, I decided it wouldn't hurt to try.

I got serious about finding answers, ran building plans by Charlie, and went to the bank for a loan. I had no experience with large loans, so I winged my presentation to the bankers by talking until I was stopped. Then I backed off, reassessed the situation, and offered more collateral.

Tenacity is the key to many things, and by the spring, all the building materials were loaded on a boat and headed for the bay. I wanted it to be up and ready by mid-July.

There were a few problems in the shipping, and I had to fly to the small town of Dillingham to correct them. On the way home, the plane stopped at all of the villages up the Nushagak River. The other passengers seemed irritated by the stops, but I was tickled pink.

At one place, I was surprised to see a young lady with her baby under her parka, flying over a snow burm on a three-wheeler. When she neared the plane, she pulled the mail sacks, gave them to the pilot, loaded the incoming mail on her machine, and flew back over the burm for her return journey. Behind her, a bright-eyed little one peeked out from beneath the parka hood. Sights like that made the trip memorable and fun.

Included in the price of the storage building was a crew to build it. When the pieces arrived at the beach, the crew went to work efficiently and effectively, and I breathed a sigh of relief over one less worry. In a few days, the building took shape, almost seeming to rise from nothing out of the tundra behind our house.

In record time, the building was finished. In final form it measured 50-by-200 feet with 18-foot sidewalls. Charlie's "cat" tractor and trailer, which would pull the boats from the water and move them into the storage building, were ready, too.

Word was out, and we were in business, except for one thing—we needed a boat to store!

We didn't have to wait long. I got a call from the *Jennifer B,* an older wooden boat with a deep draft. I was excited; it had been a long haul to get to this point. I told Charlie and he fired up the "cat," hooked onto the trailer, and went down to get the boat. But try as he might, Charlie couldn't get the boat on the

trailer. It was too far from shore for our little tractor, even though Charlie drove until the seat was floating.

So, we had to turn away our first customer.

After that, another boat came, and Charlie managed to get it on the trailer. Everything seemed like a go, but later, Charlie came into the house looking sick—the tractor barely managed to pull the boat up the hill.

This was an unexpected problem; the "cat" was tested in Homer and never showed any sign of trouble. I called the equipment company's mechanic, and his diagnosis was that our little "cat" needed a $10,000 overhaul in Anchorage. On top of that, it cost us $1,100 for him to examine the tractor and give us the bad news.

Charlie was furious. "That's it, Wil, I knew this crazy idea wouldn't work. And now we are in debt up to our eyebrows."

I wanted to cry, but as I've been known to say, you can't holler "Whoa!" in a horse race. Instead, I grabbed my coat and purse, called a plane, and headed to Anchorage.

"What are you going to do?" Charlie asked, pausing his tirade, and looking startled.

"Well, I don't really know—but I'm going to do something!"

Later that day, I went tractor shopping. I found one the same model as we had, completely rebuilt and guaranteed, for an asking price of $26,000.

Hmmm, would the company carry me?

No. They did not do financing.

I didn't want to talk to the bank; we were already stretched out with the boat storage loan. Also, anything that stopped our operation would make them nervous, and I hate nervous bankers—they are the most pessimistic people on earth.

The equipment salesman knew of an organization that financed equipment, so I went to see them. After making out the forms, answering their questions, and stressing the importance of time, I prayed a lot. Everything we owned was already borrowed against, and all I had to offer as collateral was jawbone.

I must have looked honest because I left there with the tractor I wanted—financed and delivered to the airport.

In mid-June, a young man visited us at Coffee Point. He represented a company with 17 fishing boats that needed storage.

"Would you be interested in building a second building to house them?" he asked me.

"We would consider it," I told him, "but right now financing would be a problem for us."

After some discussion, his company agreed to lend us the money. And when we finished fishing that fall, the second building was in place.

The company did not send the volume we had first expected, but we were still able to fill one building, which was enough to pay the bills. With a winter watchman hired to keep an eye on things, we breathed a sigh of relief and left the bay.

That fall, I was more tired than usual, and Charlie was a nervous wreck. Although he was an excellent loader operator, the responsibility of handling those expensive boats weighed heavily on him. After a while, he quieted down, but all winter he was moody and resented the time I spent on business. His other concern—that we had our names on so many dotted lines—was irreconcilable.

So ended 1979.

Seaside Kitchen

The new year was a very demanding time, but it was wonderful for our lives to be headed in a definite direction.

The younger kids were in school, Coni and Mike had divorced, and Tommy was bouncing around the world, foot-loose and fancy-free.

By this time, I didn't fish anymore, and there wasn't even time to help haul fish when the run hit. I missed the excitement of dragging that first full net up the beach, but I still had plenty to do.

That summer, a storm with eighty-knot winds wreaked havoc with fishing boats in the bay and many were driven ashore. Charlie had sold the *Blue Bird* to a guy in Egegik, and he needed a new boat. The *Aleutian Star* swamped two miles upriver, and I contacted the owner. The next day, the young man came by to see me at the house.

Later that afternoon I said to Charlie:

"Honey, let's go for a ride up to Bartlett's."

(You'd think by now he'd be leery of my requests for rides, but as usual, he was agreeable.)

When we spotted the boat, which sat even with the waterline in the sand, I said, "Let's go take a look."

As Charlie climbed around on the boat, Curt, the owner, came strolling by. As we talked, I made mental estimates on what it would take to restore the boat to working condition.

"I'll give you a thousand dollars for it where it sits," I offered.

Curt raised that a bit, I agreed, and I made out a check right there.

Oblivious, Charlie came over from his inspection and said:

"Boy, someone sure has their work cut out for them with this thing."

"Honey", I said, "That's you! I just bought it."

He seemed to take it well, and we went back to Coffee Point for jacks and planks to begin the first phase of the rescue effort—lifting the boat out of the mud. As the boat was elevated, the hole had appeared on the portside so awe-inspiring, Charlie started hollering at me:

"This is your damn boat—you fix it!"

But I still believed in my purchase.

"Let me run up and get Nick the fiber glass guy" I said "the Guys always say that the strongest parts of the boat are the fiber glass patches."

Charlie looked unconvinced. I wondered if I had maybe overdone a good thing.

As promised, I managed to bring Nick back with me, and after inspecting the hole he said to Charlie, "Looks like you made yourself a good deal there. That hole will patch up fine."

Charlie smiled—it was his boat again.

At the end of the summer, we hired a new watchman—my son Tommy. Almost 30 he was saving to buy his first airplane. He was enthused about his new winter job and he shipped in a new snow machine for winter transportation. We reinforced and insulated the floor in his quarters to be sure that he would be warm.

As snug as we could make him, we left Tommy to his task and headed back to Homer where we would get on with our own winter tasks of finishing up book keeping, doing taxes, and planning for the coming year.

More Changes

Pushing through the snow drifts, we opened camp at the beach in March of 1981. In general, Charlie ignored the weather, but one bi-product—blowing sand—moved him to shake out of every piece of bedding we used. Even with good insulation and tightly covered joints the new house could not protect Charlie from fine blowing sand.

In the spring I got a letter from Reenie, a young woman who had boarded with us in Homer whole attending high school. Since then she had married and moved to Washington state. The letter she wrote was heartbreaking; her husband Phil gone down on his boat in Puget Sound. He was a solid, sensible, steady person and would be missed by all who knew him.

As I continued to get ready for the season, my mind often returned to Reenie. Then it occurred to me that she was a good cook and I needed help in the kitchen. I radio Charlie's mother for help: "can you call Reenie and ask her if she would like to come to Coffee Point and cook. If she says yes tell her I will arrange a ticket for next Monday."

Awed by fast moving events, Reenie arrived on the beach the following Monday. She was not sure if Coffee Point was at the end of the world or just very close. I tried to reassure her, but the next morning, she called out to me from her bedroom.

"Wilma—Is this big brown bear supposed to be here?"

I got up and looked out her window. Sure enough, a nice-sized brown bear was breakfasting in our garbage can.

"Well, it was his country first, so we'll just have to walk around him," I laughed.

In late May, I flew to King Salmon to return an emergency call from Carmen in California. Her husband Paul had died of a heart attack. I thought frantically of how I could get away to be with her but, reading my mind, she said:

"Mom, please don't try to come. You have to cook for the crew and I'll be there soon. I know how hectic things are for you."

Two weeks later, it was a very sad girl who arrived on the beach with her three children. But Carmen is a strong person. She stayed busy, dedicated herself to her kids, and went about fishing as usual.

One foggy day, I was cooking in the kitchen when a call came over the VHF radio:

"Coffee Point, Coffee Point, this is the *Nora* calling."

I knew the voice; the man stored his boat with us.

"Yes, Roy, go ahead," I answered, turning over a hamburger on the grill.

"Wilma, we're going down."

In one motion, I flipped the hamburger off the grill, and grabbed my logbook and pencil. With no Coast Guard station close enough to assist us in emergencies, we had to help each other.

"Roy, give me your Loran coordinates," I said into the mike. "And do you have survival gear?"

"Only one survival suit and I'm putting it on Junior," he answered. His son, Junior, had rheumatoid arthritis. Without survival suits, Roy and his deckhand John would have to stay afloat by swimming.

Roy gave me the *Nora's* coordinates.

"Are you in the fog, Roy?"

"Yes, it's pea soup where I am."

"Okay, I'm going off channel for a couple of minutes to alert everybody that you need help. While I'm gone, stay on this frequency and repeat your coordinates as long as you can to see if anybody else can hear you. I'll get right back to you."

I know that Roy's heart must have been pounding, but he answered calmly:

"Okay, Wilma, later."

I stayed on the radio, bouncing from channel to channel, announcing Roy's location and saying:

"Heads up guys, we have a boat going down. Two guys without survival suits—one with."

When I got back to Roy, he was still on board, but he told me it was time to get off the boat. All I could do was wish him luck and go back to the other channels to look for help.

At that moment, the fisherman closest to Roy's coordinates, Eddie on the *Miss Lisa,* probably sighed a little as he pulled his gear. Fishermen are usually great about helping each other, but leaving a good set is against their nature.

Not long afterwards, a surprising message came through: Eddie was so close to Roy's position, John the deckhand was found clinging to the end of the *Miss Lisa's* buoy! Circling around in the fog, Eddie also picked up Roy and Junior. Unfortunately for John, when he went over the side, he slipped his glasses and $5,000 in cash inside his shirt. That was fine until he was pulled aboard the rescue boat and his shirt-tail came out. All his valuables sank to the bottom of the bay.

The men insisted on coming to Coffee Point to see me, even though I had a medic standing by in Egegik. When they arrived, Junior was fine, but John and Roy showed signs of hypothermia. After we got them warm and dry, they recovered quickly. Roy recovered so quickly that within an hour he was already concerned about getting another fishing boat. I told him there was one in storage owned by a young man without a permit. I gave Roy the young man's number, and by the next day, Roy, John and Junior were out fishing once again.

That summer, following a big storm, another boat was beached about five miles from Coffee Point, near our old house. At the time, Charlie was fishing the *Aleutian Star,* but wanted something bigger. One day, as he left to go fishing, he said: "Get that boat down the beach for me. It's called the *Impressive.*"

I was a little surprised at this and ran after him saying: "I haven't even seen it—What do you want me to bid? Who owns it?"

"Oh, I don't know, Wil. Take care of it."

It aggravated me that he hadn't given me a price. But soon, I found the owner, made a bid of $1,000, and forgot about it.

A couple of days later, I was amazed when I got a message from the owner saying; "Okay, send the check."

Once again, Charlie had a new boat, this time a twin-screw, 32-foot fishing vessel that needed work. To defray expenses, Charlie sold the *Aleutian Star* at the end of the season.

That summer, Charlie pulled the *Impressive's* engines and sent them to Homer to work on later. I ordered replacement windows and contacted a fiberglass man to repair the hull. The boat required major repairs and re-wiring, but when Charlie was finished with it, it looked great.

Around this time, more things began to change at the point. Television and video arrived, and we bought our first desperately needed automatic washer and electric dryer. As I became more tied to the kitchen and office, Charlie spent more time with other fishermen, or visiting along the beach without me. I missed the togetherness of our old way of life, but I had a job to do, and focused on that instead.

In the fall, we canned our fish, and our lives returned to normal for a brief time.

That winter, Tommy worked as our watchman again. By then he had earned enough money to buy his first airplane, a Super Cub with big tires for beach landings.

Tommy was happy, but I was scared for him. The weather in Bristol Bay was a test for both pilots and fishermen. It is only a twenty-minute flight from King Salmon to the point, but it can be very jolting when the plane is buffeted by updrafts or down drafts.

That winter, Tommy's windshield iced up on a flight, and while trying to clear it, he knocked a hole in the windshield. He had to land on a frozen lake and wedge an old jacket in the hole before continuing on to King Salmon.

Luckily, I didn't learn about it until much later.

It calmed my nerves somewhat when Tommy would call me on the phone from Naknek or King Salmon that winter. We would talk about any problems at Coffee Point, what he had been doing, what he needed me to send him, or which one of his brothers or sisters had recently contacted him. His calls were always full of enthusiasm, and I looked forward to them.

Just before Christmas, Carmen called, her voice shaking.

"What is it, honey?"

"Mom, I can't stand to have Christmas here without Paul. If I send you a ticket, would you go to Hawaii with me?"

That was an offer I couldn't refuse, and we spent a beautiful week on Maui together, catching up on our lives. But on Christmas Eve, I flew home to be with Charlie and the boys, and Carmen understood.

A Squeaky Noise

That winter, when Tommy flew in to take up his duties as watchman, he arrived with a little black-and-white kitten snuggled down in the sleeve of his flying jacket. I told Tommy about the birds and the bees, but I must have forgotten about cats, because he soon discovered that "Tyrone" was really "Tyronette."

When I arrived at the point in the spring of 1982, that kitten knew absolutely no one but Tommy. She would hiss at me, hump up, and look very threatening with her green eyes glaring. I had flown in early to relieve Tom as watchman so that he could get a brief vacation before fishing season. No sooner had my plane touched down, than Tommy was off to see the bright lights, leaving Bill Loomis—our net hanger since we built the boat storage—and me to hold down the fort.

One day I said to Bill:

"Have you seen the cat recently?"

"No, I guess I haven't."

"Hmm, I hope she hasn't run off. That would really upset TomTom."

By evening, I had taken several quick looks around with no luck, deciding that the cat knew her way around.

After dinner, I said to Bill:

"Maybe I ought to walk around the buildings and play watchman."

Bill offered to go with me, and together we strolled toward the boat storage, chatting.

Suddenly, I looked at him.

"What was that sound?"

I thought I'd heard a squeaky noise, and once I mentioned it, Bill heard it too.

We looked around, listening closely, until we located Tyrone, tangled hopelessly in an old fish net, lying on a frozen puddle. Her eyes were glazed; in trying to escape from the net, she had worn the skin off her legs in places.

Bill took out his knife and cut her free from her lacy prison. Poor baby, she didn't even have the strength to hiss. Holding her in my arms, we walked back to the house, where I petted her, and cleaned the bloody spots on her legs. Talking gently, I tried to soothe her after her terrible ordeal.

Since she was too weak to eat on her own, I found an eye-dropper and coaxed warm milk down her sore throat. At first, I fed her every hour, day and night, but in a couple of days, she could drink by herself. Crawling off, she managed to find a secluded spot on the top shelf of my storeroom to rest and recover.

She began to like me better after that, and we were even forming a lasting bond. Once she accepted me, she felt she had a right to lie across my bookkeeping ledger. In the late evenings, when things were quiet, she would wiggle around licking my hands until I would stop my book work and hold her.

Holding Tyrone was the one really relaxing time of my day.

We had an extremely busy summer at the bay that year. All the kids brought their families, and several times we managed to get everyone in one place for dinner.

Tommy was running a boat we had bought from Dean Wallace, and was making plans to buy a new one.

Coni, Tammy, and their families all fished our old sites at the other end of the beach. Terrill fished with Charlie on the

Impressive, and brought his young son along to meet his cousins and stay with me. Carmen, David and Brad fished Coffee Point, as usual.

Things, in general, were getting a little more organized. We hired a cook in the restaurant so that I could spend more time in the office, which had grown into a full-time job.

That winter, instead of acting as watchman, Tommy put a pack on his back and wandered off to Australia. Periodically, we'd receive calls from him, usually describing how much fun he was having and all the wonderful people he was meeting.

Stand Up Tall

Our most demanding problem in 1983 was the need for additional housing for crew and trade people. We decided to build a 16-by-60 building, two floors high, which we would call "The Hotel."

When I arrived at the point, Charlie and his crew had completed the building, and it looked practical for our needs, but it was sitting on a stack of 2-by-4s. I wondered if it would withstand the heavy Bristol Bay winds.

"Charlie, this building has a lot of surface, and it's very high. What can we do to make sure it stays put in a bad wind?"

He laughed at my anxiety and said, "Honey, you worry too much."

"Okay, but how about humoring me a little and guying it down better?

"All right," he answered, "Just as soon as I get time."

Just before lunch one day, the wind blew with such a vengeance I could hear it hammering the surface of the hotel. We had a lot of dollars invested in that building, and our crew relied on it to live in, so I went to Charlie with the problem:

"Honey, we haven't secured the hotel yet. Maybe you should get a cable and anchor the building to something since there hasn't been time to guy it properly."

Charlie was irritated with me, and I knew it from the degree of enthusiasm with which he closed the door. But soon I heard the "cat" tractor at work, and breathed a little easier—Charlie was tackling the problem.

During lunch, we heard a loud thud. What I had feared had happened; the building had come off the blocks and was tilted forward. I ran to see why the cable had not helped and found that Charlie's "quick fix" was a springy nylon line tied to the "cat" that stretched under pressure, allowing the building to fall off its shaky pillars.

Now, there were two of us who were not happy.

The restaurant was doing well enough that the addition we built to enlarge it was inadequate. Charlie and I decided that our best option was to move the cafe into our house on Alder Way. By then, the kids had all built houses of their own along the beach, and the extra bedrooms would require little remodeling to turn into an eating area.

It was a big project, but before the salmon run hit, we held a grand opening of the new and improved "Seaside Kitchen." Over 125 people attended the festivities which featured the Coffee Point favorite—a style show with the girls modeling rubber gloves and rain gear. Buddy, one of the Pen Air pilots, played guitar for us, Tommy scored some halibut, and one of the deckhands from Hawaii taught several girls how to do the hula.

Charlie and I both felt relieved, happy, and ready for the new season.

That summer, I began to spend lots of time on the radio. By then, I was working three types: a CB, a VHF and a single-sideband. It amused people to watch me at work—a mike in each hand and another on stand by—as I took orders for hamburgers, noted down instructions about picking up gear from a boat, or wrote down details about delivering an anchor up river. As I worked, I generated piles of sticky notes, tacking them on the wall in front of me until I could take care of them later.

But being on the radio was only part of my duties. My day usually started at 6 a.m. when I'd give Charlie a call if he was out fishing. Then I would do some odd jobs, go to the kitchen and get a cup of tea, jot down supply orders from my staff, and go back to the radio for my prearranged morning talk with my mother-in-law. By 8 a.m., I would settle down to book work, deal with people who came to the office, and meet planes. I closed the office during the lunch hour for a brief break.

All day and evening, I shuttled people to and from planes, made out fishing licenses, or delivered crews to their boats. By midnight, I could usually close the door to the office and head to bed.

Overall, there was little time for fun, but we were making progress toward our financial goals, and that made it worthwhile.

That fall we didn't hurry home. We fall-fished, smoked and canned fish for Homer, and got to all the projects Charlie and I had set aside during the busy days of summer.

By October 19th, word was out that we were leaving for the season, and we had a house full of company. The first snowflakes of winter were already falling. As always, I experienced a bit of culture shock leaving the peace and quiet of the bay for the noise and bustle of civilization.

Back in Homer, Charlie was in a strange mood. I figured that, like me, he was tired from a particularly trying season. He didn't seem interested in talking to me anymore, and when I asked his opinion about business things, he would say:

"You figure it out."

Finally, I gave up trying, and made the necessary decisions.

That winter Tommy married Jill, who also fished Bristol Bay, in a gala wedding in Anchorage. It seemed strange to watch my Tommy, the free spirit, making a commitment to settle down.

In the spring, Charlie went back to the beach early, and in May, he told me that the freighter had delivered the building materials for Coffee Point Store, our latest project. I was at the beach cooking for the crew when I got word that my father was hospitalized in Kirkland, Washington. I flew to see him, but two days later, he passed away.

After the funeral, Charlie met me at the plane, but didn't have much to say. To get through that very difficult season, I tried to remember my Dad's words to me: "You stand up tall and put one foot ahead of the other till the day is over."

A Kiss Good-Bye

One morning in mid-February, 1986, my mother's intuition at work, I woke up with the sudden urge to visit TomTom in Anchorage. Although surprised by my plan, Charlie gave it his blessing. The last night of my visit, Tommy's friend came over with slides of a trip to Ireland. Tom especially enjoyed the pictures; he walked up to the screen, studying it intently like he wanted to walk into the picture. It was a wonderful evening, and when it came to a close, I noticed my son starting up the stairs, carrying his new little boy.

"Hey, Tommy," I said, "I'll probably head home before you get up in the morning—so, where's my kiss?" He laughed, hugged and kissed me, and said he'd see me when he got back from Coffee Point where he would be delivering a three-wheeler for one of his sisters.

At about 4 p.m. the next day, the thought of Tommy popped into my mind, and I figured he was about to call me.

But no call came.

That evening, Tommy's wife Jill called me. In a tight little voice, she said:

"Wilma, something strange just happened."

"What is that, Jill?" I asked.

"They just lost Tommy off the radar."

"Where?" I came back quickly.

"Over Turnagain Arm, about seven minutes out."

My heart plummeted. There it was. The one thing I had always feared when Tom flew his plane.

"Jill, please keep me posted," I said.

She hung up with a quick, "Okay."

I pulled out the desk drawer and opened a tide book. Top of a thirty-foot tide, icebergs floating everywhere in the water, the weather dark and snowing.

Oh, Tom, no, my heart cried out.

On the return trip from King Salmon, flying his beloved Cessna 206, our Tommy disappeared. On that fateful night, the country my son loved so much simply swallowed him up, leaving no trace.

On My Own

That fall, as we all struggled with the loss of Tommy, Charlie and I marked our 25th wedding anniversary.

"Gee, honey," I said. "We've made it a quarter of a century."

Charlie looked at me oddly, but his expression did not prepare me for his next statement:

"Yes—And we're not going any further."

Could this be happening? I guess it's something that had been coming for a long time, but I just hadn't wanted to see it.

I had always thought that suicide was for deranged people, but to me, it seemed logical under the circumstances. I was alone for the first time in many years, and my house, which had held all the sounds of growing children, was totally quiet. Friends and family rallied, making sure I didn't spend much time by myself. And on a particularly low day, Brad brought me a single yellow rose in a tiny vase, and not long after, arranged a trip to Ireland for me.

Somehow, instead of planning my demise, I clung to life instead. When Brad told me how important it was for me to be at his high school graduation, it moved me to think more about the future.

Just before the trip to Ireland, I stopped at Tammy's in Maryland. Together, we walked along the Chester River, watching the sailboats and eating delicious crab cakes at a nearby restaurant. Life was looking up, and I knew then there were many wonderful things I still had to do.

Epilogue

The Good Land

In 1990 I sold Coffee Point, but every year I make a trip back, staying in a little house Tommy built overlooking Egegik Bay. From there, I look out over the tender boats and fishing fleet and enjoy the sights that for so many years, have been an important part of my life.

When I'm at the bay, I often see Charlie, who still fishes on the *Impressive.* We don't talk much, although we still have David and Brad in common, and sometimes it feels strange to see him living a life apart from mine.

Year round, I live in the tiny hamlet of Homer, and I actually have time to plant flowers and visit with my children and their families. Coni lives in Homer and helps her husband with his construction company. Brad, who speaks fluent Japanese, is a travel agent and still fishes a site at Coffee Point. Terrill is a mechanic, and his daughter, Alissa, was recently voted Miss Preteen of Alaska. Tammy and her husband, John, manage their family rentals in Maryland.

Carmen, who is a vascular technician in Bellingham, Washington, has visited China and Australia. She always returns from her travels with wonderful stories. David has a new wife and daughter, fishes every season, and works in Seattle as a carpenter.

And above us all, our Tommy watches over us from beyond the earthly curtain:

> *Some say God was tired when He made it;*
> *Some say it's a good land to shun;*
> *Maybe; but there's some as would trade it*
> *For no land on earth—and I'm one.*
>
> —Robert Service

10998358R10065

Printed in Great Britain
by Amazon